My Life with Cranes

By
George Archibald

Edited by Betsy Didrickson

INTERNATIONAL CRANE FOUNDATION

Published by and available from:
The International Crane Foundation
E11376 Shady Lane Road
Baraboo, WI 53913 USA
www.savingcranes.org

All proceeds from the sale of this book
benefit global crane conservation efforts by the
International Crane Foundation.

My Life with Cranes
By George Archibald
Copyright © 2016 International Crane Foundation
Second printing
All Rights Reserved
Edited by Betsy Didrickson
Design by Jay Jocham, LooseAnimals.com

ISBN 978-0-9979405-0-3

DEDICATION

This book is dedicated to
the two ladies who cared for me
throughout most of my life,
my mother, Annie Leticia Archibald,
and my lovely wife,
Kyoko Matsumoto Archibald.

George Archibald

As the rain poured down, and with the darkness shattered only by lightning, I carried Tex gently in my arms down the grassy hill from our shared nest. When I spoke her name, she responded with low soft purring sounds that seemed to confirm a sense of security. Holding one of the last remaining Whooping Cranes on earth during that violent storm, I felt a powerful bond with her and to cranes everywhere. My unusual pair bond with Tex became well known in those early days and garnered awareness for her species – but for me – the story of Tex will always be a metaphor for the complicated dance performed by many to help save one of the world's most threatened family of birds.

Contents

FOREWORD

A Life with Cranes

By Jim Harris, International Crane Foundation, Senior Vice President

For all of us who love listening to George and his stories, here is a birthday gift we can accept with both hands. Reading these uplifting, sometimes strange memories, we glimpse the uncertainty and clouds of threat that surrounded this magnificent and imperiled family of birds. Threats remain, but today it is difficult to imagine the world George saw forty years ago in the formative years of the International Crane Foundation (ICF). Russia and China remained off limits to western conservationists, so that fieldwork was not possible across vast and critical habitats for five threatened crane species. Captive breeding and species banks offered little for cranes as a backup survival strategy. At that time, North American zoos held just four Red-crowned Cranes in total (two males in Massachusetts and two females in Hawaii), and one aged Siberian Crane. Among threatened species, few cranes had ever bred in captivity.

George is a great storyteller, true stories that he himself made happen through faith and perseverance. These qualities kept George going despite numerous setbacks – the disease disaster for the captive flock, the loss of Tex the Whooping Crane to a mob of raccoons, and the unexpected death of George's close friend and conservation partner Ron Sauey, on a Christmas morning. Time and again, George dared act. This volume offers many examples. Here is one we can savor: imagine taking the public bus across Iran accompanied only by a handful of cards bearing simple phrases in Persian, a short time later walking alone through rain and mud among the rice paddies toward a damgah (duck trap) in order to locate Siberian Cranes – only to be intercepted by stern hunters who didn't welcome strangers. Yet just at that moment, you might be able to guess whose loud calls rose from behind the line of trees and waterfowl traps. But there is an even more satisfying question – who else but George would walk into such a situation? Each such a gamble… like his impossible journey during the "Wet" through the Australian Outback… or a moment one October, dejected by the futility of his search for cranes inside the supremely dangerous Demilitarized Zone of Korea. At that moment, he turned to his only companion, his Korean soldier bodyguard, "What should I do?"

For over forty years, we have loved retelling the moment when two graduate students discovered their dream of an international center for the study and preservation of cranes. George recalls a restaurant where he and Ron first seized upon this vision. The bitter wind and snowflakes flying that afternoon in upstate New York, in what Ron called a bar that warmed their chilled limbs, warmed the stirrings of their dream. George and Ron never turned back.

Some may read these stories hoping to know George better, or to glimpse what has made his lifelong achievements possible. This volume gives instance after instance of leaps of faith, a tireless ambitious search for meaningful action. Or said another way, the passionate readiness to leap for opportunity… to enter China, or Russia to create close friendships that enabled the complexities of 10,000-mile egg shipments to happen during the dark years of the cold war.

Most of the stories come from the early years, when dreaming big depended on taking risks and on the freedom to follow creativity. Perhaps George has chosen these stories, out of many that deserve telling, because listeners have always favored them. We love to recall how the International Crane Foundation rose and grew despite all odds. George has always offered hope.

My favorite passage appears near the end, when a close friend gives George simple advice for how he might choose to spend his years after this 70th birthday. We glimpse an introspective George, a man accustomed to think and look within. And what he offers brings the larger story full circle, to give his time, his encouragement to helping others – young men and women – live their own versions of dream and action. Ultimately, George has succeeded through the trust we have all afforded him for his immense caring, for the cranes certainly, and for all of us.

August 1952. New trailer.

Early Days in Canada

IMPRINTING

My first memory is of golden sunlight on green grass and a brown mother duck and her brood of yellow ducklings. Too young to walk, I crawled after the brood. My friends claim I imprinted on birds then, and have been following them ever since. My second memory is of feeding colored coconut to domestic ducks in Sherbrooke, Nova Scotia, Canada, and my third memory is one of anger after having discovered several wild ducks that my father had shot hanging in the back porch. One thing is certain, my earliest memories are of birds, and since childhood, I have had a passionate interest in nature, and birds in particular.

My loving parents, Donald and Lettie Archibald, recognized and appreciated this special interest of their little son. Both were teachers who shared an interest in learning and nature. Dad loved farming, fishing and hunting, while Mom was a skilled gardener. Our rural home bordering a small field beside the St. Mary's River was surrounded by wilderness from which deer, moose, bears and eagles sometimes appeared. Our field provided pasture for a cow, a horse, and space for a large vegetable garden.

VICTOR BAKHTIN

James. 8 mile brook 1955

I am the second born of six children – 2 girls and 4 boys. My siblings and I shared close relationships with each other and with nature, expressed in different degrees by gardening, farming, fishing, and hunting. I was the only one captivated by birds. My brother Don once commented that I was fortunate to have a strong passion in something that provided such a clear direction. My siblings all flourished – Anne the English teacher, Don the carpenter, Heather the primary school teacher and later in business, Sandy and his three sons – all Royal Canadian Mounted Police, and Peter the agro-businessman in Newfoundland.

Peter, in his early teens, came to Cornell and later to Baraboo, Wisconsin in the summers to share quality time with me and to help care for the cranes. We were very close. In 1981, he was the best man at my wedding. In February of 2005, while leading a group of ICF members in Japan, I received a call that Peter (then 46) had suddenly passed away from a ruptured aorta. Unable to leave the group, I somehow completed the tour while phoning family each night. That May, I spent a week with Peter's family to plant the gardens and share memories of someone deeply loved by many.

Aside from a grandmother of British stock, I am primarily of Scottish descent. My ancestors, the Archibalds and MacLeods, left Scotland for a better life in Canada. The Archibalds arrived in Nova Scotia in the late 1700s and the MacLeods in 1804. It is a joy that my first cousin, Alexander

MacLeod continues to farm the land that was homesteaded by our immigrant ancestors. My parents embraced the traditional Scottish value of thrift. Wash water was never discarded but used to water the gardens. Three small sheds that others would have destroyed were transported to our property and neatly placed beside the forest. They became homes for my menagerie of birds, including peafowl, pheasants, chickens, geese, ducks, and pigeons. Despite their limited financial resources, my parents graciously purchased food for the many hungry avian mouths. I inherited the frugal gene from my parents, which later came in handy during the lean, early years of establishing a non-profit organization.

My own first birds during childhood were four Rhode Island Red laying hens, followed by five white leghorns reared from eggs and hatched by a broody hen. The chicks developed into three hens and two handsome and ferocious roosters. To promote domestic peace in the chicken house, Dad butchered one of the roosters. I was upset and pled the case that chickens might someday become endangered! I was sad that chickens seemed unable to fly long distances, and I wanted to help them. So, I carried them to the roof of the barn and after they recovered from the stress of transport, I pushed them off. Alas, they did not progress well in flight and undoubtedly, their egg production was curtailed by this flight therapy. It brought me hours of great joy to watch the behavior of my domestic birds. Hens returning to roost in the evening fascinated me, as each selected its own special spot on the perch. Why the same spot I wondered? And why did people always sit in the same seat in church?

In autumn and spring, a flock of wild Canada Geese flew over our valley with raucous calls that stirred my spirit. In the forest, I was thrilled to discover the nests or broods of Ruffed Grouse. Fishermen would sometimes leave me for hours on coastal islands to search for nests of Eider Ducks, Common Terns, Herring and Black-backed Gulls, and Double-crested Cormorants. Occasionally, I brought home a few eggs from these wild birds and hatched them under chickens. The young were hand-reared and then released back into the wild. I have fond memories of newly fledged terns and gulls flying down to grab food from my uplifted hands. It brought me a deep sense of satisfaction that the captive-reared birds became wild and free.

During these formative years, I did not have much exposure to small birds. The feeding of wild birds in winter was not practiced by anyone I knew. I did not have binoculars or a field guide and little birds were difficult to see. Years later, I discovered I was color blind, a handicap that legitimized my inability to discern many shades in those "little brown jobs." Large birds were easy to identify and as a project in biology class, I compiled a ring binder on the waterfowl of North America.

While growing up, perhaps the greatest thrill was a visit every few years to the Provincial Wildlife Park near Shubenacadie, Nova Scotia. Mammals and birds could be seen alive and up close. Canada Geese and Wood Ducks flew to and from the ponds at the Park to convey a lovely blend of the wild and captive environment. Eldon Pace, the creator and manager of the Park, subsequently became a mentor and life-long friend. He helped me realize the importance of captive animals in cultivating the interest of young people in the appreciation and conservation of nature.

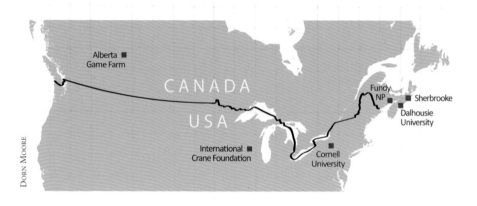

FLEDGING

Except for a pair of peafowl, my childhood bird collection was dispersed to others after I graduated from high school. I intended to become a medical doctor and pursued pre-medical studies through a Bachelor of Science in biology and chemistry at Dalhousie University in Halifax. During my undergraduate years, I dedicated summer vacations to earning income from jobs related to nature. The first summer I raised and released Mallard Ducks and banded Black Ducks for the provincial government on the Nova Scotia estate of American business tycoon, Cyrus Eaton.

The Eaton Estate was run a bit like Downton Abby with administrators, cooks, gardeners, drivers, and Mr. Eaton's personal secretary, Ray Szabo. My life-long friendship with the Szabo family started that summer, and through Ray, this young man from the back woods of Nova Scotia learned much about the ways of contemporary aristocrats, lessons that proved very useful a few years later when I needed to cultivate people to help secure support for crane conservation.

The following two summers, I was employed to study and care for cranes and other birds at Al Oeming's Alberta Game Farm. There in the northwest, I was uplifted to experience Sandhill Cranes in the wild and interacted with eight species of captive cranes that I fed and watered daily. Through Al's deep passion for cranes and with his enthusiastic support, my interest in

conservation grew. I knew cranes were special, but why? Was it their rarity? Was it that some species are as tall as humans? Or, was it because they are monogamous and pairs dance together and call in synchronized duets? I was fascinated that the calls of migrating Sandhills were heard before the birds could be spotted through binoculars in those cold blue spring skies in Alberta. Al's enthusiasm was contagious – I was hooked!

Although I adored the wildlife park in Nova Scotia and the game farm in Alberta, and was inspired by Eldon Pace and Al Oeming, deep down I wanted more than captive animals could offer. Unaware of the possibility of ornithology as a profession, I decided on medicine as a career and birds as a hobby. After all these big decisions had been made, in November of 1967 in the company of a close friend and colleague, Tim Tuff (who in 2014 became a member of the Board of Directors of the International Crane Foundation),

I attended the world's fair in Montreal. After one day of doing the tourist thing, I decided to hitchhike south to Ithaca, New York to visit the famed Laboratory of Ornithology at Cornell University. It was there I met a man who changed my life, Professor William Dilger.

KINDRED SPIRITS

On that cold November day in 1967, I walked the corridors of the Cornell Laboratory of Ornithology, admired the original bird paintings by Louis Agassiz Fuertes, and then heard the distinct sound of parrots. At the end of a long, dark corridor, bright light and birdcalls poured from an open door. Timidly I walked into a room filled with cages of small colorful parrots. This room led to the office of Professor Dilger, an ethologist at Cornell University, best known for his behavior studies on parrots, and for providing scientific insight into the age-old controversy between nature verses nurture. Surprised to see an unannounced stranger, Professor Dilger invited me to join him for a chat. Dressed in leather lederhosen and smoking a long, curved Burmese pipe, Dilger immediately put me at ease by requesting I address him by his first name, Bill (a custom not practiced at Dalhousie). During the next hour, I had the undivided attention of a kindred spirit as I shared my knowledge of cranes with a truly eccentric individual in a colorful office filled with books, papers, aquaria, and birdcages. Without asking the typical questions about background and achievements, Bill invited me to come to Cornell to study cranes. Without a thought, I nodded. We hugged and I told him I hoped to start as his graduate student in September of 1968.

I had already received a National Research Council fellowship from the Canadian Government to pursue postgraduate studies for five years. I had elected to become a pediatrician by attending the Medical School at Dalhousie University. Accepted and with full financial backing, my destiny seemed secure. Leaving Ithaca, I reasoned, I would use my fellowship to study cranes rather than kids! Within a few months, Cornell accepted me, I sent the medical school my regrets, and started thinking in high gear about cranes and conservation.

That last summer in Canada, under the supervision of gifted naturalist David Christie, I became a seasonal park naturalist at magnificent Fundy National Park. It was a total delight to share with visitors the world's highest tides and the brilliant abundance of songbirds in the Acadian forests. David taught me two important skills: how to identify tiny songbirds and how to speak effectively in public. I found it difficult to believe I was being paid to have so much fun. It was a dream job! But I was in for a great shock. I had failed to read the fine print in the letter from the National Research Council announcing my fellowship. It stated this support from the Canadian Government could only be used at a Canadian institution. Cornell was in the United States. Shocked and dismayed, I called Bill for advice. He replied, "To hell with it. Come anyway, George. We'll find something." His magnetic personality and great warmth bolstered me. At the end of that summer, I was sad to leave my country, my family, and my friends, with only $800 (Canadian) to my name. But I knew I had made the right decision, so off I went to the United States.

The Cornell Cranium

In September of 1968, I arrived at the expensive Ivy League school literally penniless. In my naivety about travel, I had placed my wallet in my suitcase. To this day, that suitcase has never been located. Fortunately, David Williams, Director of the Foreign Student Office, loaned me a few hundred dollars for food and clothes, and got me situated in a dormitory. My major professor, Bill Dilger, helped me land a research assistantship at Cornell's Laboratory for Ornithology, support that provided both tuition and a respectable salary. Actually, I was able to save money while at Cornell, a small fund that helped me four years later through the early lean years at the International Crane Foundation.

The Lab is in the countryside several miles from Cornell's main campus complex in Ithaca, New York. The first two years, I lived on campus and commuted to the Lab by bus and later by my first car, a 1965 Falcon. My goal was to establish a captive population of cranes at the Lab to conduct a comparative study of their behavioral displays. Within a week of my arrival, I started to prepare for the arrival of cranes. A small pond in a weed-filled field across the road from the Lab was soon fenced and an abandoned shed dragged to the site to provide shelter for two female Sandhill Cranes from the Alberta Game Farm. In another field stood an abandoned complex which until recently had been the site of Cornell's mink research. I secured the mink complex at the suggestion of another mentor, Professor Tom Cade. It would all soon become the home for 56 cranes. It was also home for me and my Labrador retriever, Fuji. The dilapidated buildings were scheduled to be leveled at the end of 1971, so I only had them for three years.

My summer of 1969 was dedicated to the removal of rows of mink cages, many of which I sold and used the funds to excavate ponds and build high fences for cranes. The old office building provided a room for food storage, two rooms in winter for the cold sensitive crowned cranes from Africa, and one small room for Fuji and me. To make my space feel larger, I installed a large picture window (found at the local dump) to provide a commanding view of the enclosure for Wattled Cranes. My next objective was to secure cranes and funds to care for them, at what soon became known as the *Cornell Cranium*.

WHO DO YOU THINK YOU ARE?

At that time, Dr. Sewall Pettingill was the Director of the Laboratory for Ornithology. Some years prior to his arrival at Cornell, he was involved in a search for the then unknown nesting grounds of the Whooping Cranes in northern Canada. He knew cranes, and he was considered royalty in the academic community. One day, he asked to see me in his office. He questioned the wisdom of my interest in developing a large captive collection of cranes at Cornell. "Cranes are well known and highly respected. If things do not go well, it will not be the best reflection on the Lab." I assured him of my dedication and competence to manage the project. He remained reflective with a definite twinkle of support in his conservative eyes. Another member of my graduate committee was Professor Oliver Hewitt (Ollie). Ollie was a tiny man with a warm heart, who had access to a fleet of university vehicles! Enthused about my dreams, he agreed to provide vans and fuel to fetch cranes for the *Cranium*.

The next step in my efforts to gain support for my project was to visit the Bronx Zoo office of the highly respected Dr. William Conway, Director of the prestigious New York Zoological Society. While I explained the project, Dr. Conway remained silent but attentive. Then he cleared his throat, stared at me, and said, "Who do you think you are? Cranes are revered, costly, and rare birds that require top-level professional management. You have a heavy academic program to face. How can you possibly care for so many cranes with zero financial resources?" I calmly replied that I had 22 years of living with birds, I had raised Sandhills and cared for eight species of cranes at the Alberta Game Farm, and that I was willing to live with the cranes, study them, raise funds to support them, and complete my doctorate concurrently. Unmoved, he asked me if I would like to join him on a walk around the zoo. On that walk we talked and soon discovered that we indeed were kindred spirits – his doubts about me seemed to melt away. Before departing the zoo that day, I had the promise of $5,000 cash for the Cornell Crane Research Project, and one female White-naped, two Eurasians, two Blue, two Grey Crowned, four Sarus, and six Demoiselle Cranes. I was in crane heaven!

CHIMBA AND RORY

During our walk around the Bronx Zoo that memorable day, Dr. Conway and I encountered a seemingly human-imprinted female White-naped Crane named Chimba, with a bent wing, many broken feathers, and bald areas from feather picking. Alone in an off-exhibit area near the African Plains, she was pacing the fence trying to join us. I felt a great sympathy for her, and soon she was on the list of cranes to migrate to Cornell for a few years. She was so tame and gentle on the trip north, I opened the top of her shipping crate so she could stick her neck out of the partly opened window. The startled attendant at the tollgate jumped back when she blinked!

I placed her alone in a large grassy paddock with a small pond, and three pre-fledged, wild-caught Sandhills as neighbors. When I noticed that Chimba was feeding the Sandhills grasshoppers through the wire, I knew I had a "family." The fence was removed and the four cranes lived together. The wild-caught cranes, accustomed to following their natural parents, soon were following Chimba. Chimba became a new bird. She went through a molt of wing and body feathers and emerged an elegant crane with a slightly bent wing. She was gorgeous. Despite not having a mate, but with three adopted juveniles, the next spring she laid five eggs! The Memphis Zoo had a lone male named Rory, and he was sent to pair with Chimba. Unfortunately, getting Rory to the *Cranium* was not without complications.

One autumn morning in 1969, Rory was to be air freighted to Syracuse (40 miles north of the *Cranium*) via a connecting flight at LaGuardia Airport in New York. When he did not arrive as expected in Syracuse, I called the Memphis Zoo and confirmed the shipping number and other details. They assured me that he had departed for New York. The staff at LaGuardia, however, repeatedly informed me that there was no record of the crane. There was nothing to do but to drive to New York. It was late evening when I finally arrived at the cargo bay of La Guardia Airport. Five men were playing cards under a hanging light bulb in a dimly lit, dusty room. They rudely informed me, as they had by phone that the crane was not there! I asked if I might look for her in the bowels of the cargo storage area just beyond the card game. "Absolutely not! This is a highly restricted area." Exasperated, I sat down and stewed for a while. Finally, I jumped to my feet, walked past the card game and proceeded into the storage area. No one tried to stop me and within a few minutes, I located the crate with Rory. He had been without food or water since early morning.

My aunt and uncle, John and Delores Archibald, lived in a beautiful condo in Port Chester, about 40 miles from the airport. I called Aunt Del and explained the crisis. It was after midnight when I placed Rory's crate on a large piece of plastic atop pristine white carpet in the middle of Aunt Del's

MY LIFE WITH CRANES

living room. I removed the top of the crate and placed a bucket of water beside the weakened crane. He immediately started to drink. I felt he was too weak to escape, so, exhausted myself, I went to bed leaving the top of the crate open. The next morning, my Uncle John woke early and came downstairs. Unaware of the events of the previous evening, he was shocked to discover a huge bird peering over the top of a four-foot high plywood box in his living room!

LOVE AT FIRST SIGHT

It was love at first sight. Chimba and Rory paired immediately, and the next spring she laid 12 eggs. Unfortunately, they were infertile, but the following spring she laid 12 more eggs. Five of these hatched in the massive incubator at Cornell's Poultry Science Department. Unfortunately, two of the chicks were born blind. I named them Helen and Keller, and two years later they were the first cranes to arrive in Baraboo at the newly formed International Crane Foundation.

In the autumn of 1971, Chimba, Rory, and their five youngsters along with many other cranes were delivered to the Bronx Zoo when the *Cranium* was disassembled. Bill Conway's investment had been a productive one. Chimba and Rory produced many offspring over subsequent decades. Their breeding was the beginning of a major inter-zoo program in the U.S. to establish a viable population of White-naped Cranes in captivity. Fast-forward 30 years – as I was touring the Bronx Zoo with two colleagues from Bhutan, I was delighted to discover that Chimba was alive and well and

paired with a new mate following the passing of Rory some years before. When I walked into her enclosure, she walked up to me and stood beside me. I gave her a hug. My colleagues were both amazed and deeply touched – and so was I.

JOHN FORD

THE UNISON CALL

I soon assembled a collection of 56 cranes of nine species (on loan from the government, zoos, and private individuals) including the Black Crowned, Grey Crowned, Demoiselle, Blue, Wattled, Sandhill, Sarus, White-naped, and Eurasian. With subjects on hand at the *Cranium*, I was now able to focus on my research. I observed three other species, Hooded, Red-crowned, and Whooping Cranes, at other centers in the Northeast. I analyzed the behavior of the Brolga from films and sound recordings taken by Australian colleagues, but unfortunately, information was lacking for the Siberian and Black-necked Cranes. There was only a single Siberian Crane in captivity in the U.S. and there were no known Black-necked Cranes in captivity outside of China, which was locked in the throes of the Cultural Revolution.

Cranes are social and communicative birds whose behavior can be divided into two categories: vocal and visual. With an excellent tape recorder on loan from Cornell's Library of Natural Sounds, I recorded the calls from each species. Using a small Super 8 mm movie camera, I filmed the repertoire of threat postures and dances. The volume of recorded information influenced me to concentrate my analysis on the comparative evolutionary relationships of cranes based on a single display – the dramatic unison call – a duet performed by a mated pair of cranes.

Male and female cranes look alike. Males are sometimes larger. Unable to determine gender by outward appearance, zoos often unknowingly paired cranes of the same gender together. At the *Cranium*, I made an interesting discovery that the sex of crane species, except for crowned cranes, can be determined by the unison call display. During this display, which signals both mate fidelity and aggression toward others, the male crane typically elevates his wings and gives one long call for two higher-pitched calls of the female. It is an easy way to tell the boys from the girls, and thus an important tool in captive management.

As I continued my research at Cornell on the vocal repertoire of the 13 available crane species, a review of the literature indicated that Wattled Cranes were quite silent compared to other cranes. Mine certainly were. I recorded low, purr-like contact calls between my mated pair, and abrupt,

loud, high-frequency flight intention calls, and when alarmed, they emitted a loud, piercing guard call – but never a unison call. What was wrong with my Wattleds?

One night at about 3:00 a.m., I was awakened by a screaming call from outside my bedroom at the *Cranium*. I scrambled to the enclosure of the Wattled Cranes to check for a predator, but the cranes stood silently beside their pond. I went back to bed, but the next night I heard the same thing. To solve the mystery, I borrowed a tape recorder from the Cornell's Library of Natural Sounds, and I recorded all the sounds from darkness until dawn. Eventually, I captured the strange calls from the Wattled Crane pen. My analysis of the call revealed a duet initiated by the female, with the male joining in unison. I had recorded the then unknown unison call of the Wattled Crane. Eventually, they performed the display more frequently and on one occasion, I filmed it at dawn.

By comparing the dozens of characteristics of the unison call among the 13 species of cranes in my study, I projected a model of their evolutionary relationships. My observations suggested that crowned cranes were the most primitive cranes. The other cranes fell into five groups: the Whooping Crane group (Whooping, Red-crowned, Hooded, and Eurasian); the Sarus group (Sarus, Brolga, and White-naped); the Demoiselle group (Demoiselle and Blue); and the Sandhill and Wattled, each separate from the others. Twenty-five years later, Dr. Carey Krajewski compared the DNA of all 15 species of cranes from blood samples collected from birds at the International Crane Foundation. The model projected by that DNA study was nearly identical to the model revealed by my behavioral research many years earlier.

I maintained a close friendship with Bill Dilger until he passed away in 2015 at the age of 92. The same year I started the *Cranium*, Tom Cade built the Peregrine Place at the Laboratory of Ornithology and started his well-known Peregrine Fund through which many gorgeous raptors have been returned as breeding residents in the lower 48 states. Just as the *Cranium* transformed into the International Crane Foundation in Wisconsin in 1973, the Peregrine Place became the World Center for the Birds of Prey in Idaho. Both projects had their beginnings in the same year at the same place – the Cornell Laboratory for Ornithology. Thank you, Cornell!

An observatory for visitors at the Laboratory for Ornithology looked out through large picture windows to bird feeders, a pond, and forest. Calls of wild birds were recorded by microphones under the eaves and amplified for visitors in the observatory. The *Cranium* was several hundred yards away through a patch of alders from the Lab. From 1969 through the autumn of 1971, the calls of cranes frequently enhanced the visitor's experience and if you were there during wee hours of the morning, you might have heard the Wattled Cranes.

It was great fun caring for the cranes, learning about their communication systems, and piecing together what the data suggested about their evolutionary relationships. Often I discussed my findings with my colleagues at Cornell and with Bill Conway at the Bronx Zoo. One day, Bill commented to me that I would be wasting my life if I pursued a career in academia. I was needed on the battleground of conservation. I was intrigued, but how was that to be expressed after completing my doctorate? Perhaps I could work for the New York Zoological Society and try to do for rare birds what George Schaller was doing for endangered mammals.

NO MERE BIRD

Aldo Leopold's, *A Sand County Almanac,* written in Wisconsin during the 1930s and 1940s, was a profound introduction to conservation for me. Leopold expressed in words how I felt about cranes.

> *When we hear his call, we hear no mere bird. We hear the trumpet in the orchestra of evolution. He is the symbol of our untamable past, of that incredible sweep of millennia which underlies and conditions the daily affairs of birds and men. The sadness discernible in some marshes arises, perhaps, from their once having harbored cranes. Now they stand humbled, adrift in history.*

MY LIFE WITH CRANES

I was deeply moved by Leopold's sentiments about cranes, feelings confirmed by replies to letters I wrote to ornithologists overseas. I was seeking information about the status of the world's cranes. Many responded that little was known about cranes and that the last observations had been many years before. Perhaps the cranes of Asia and Africa were exposed to the same pressures that reduced the Whooping Cranes in North America to fewer than 20 birds in 1940.

Knowing that my *Cornell Cranium* would be leveled in December of 1971, I applied for a grant from the New York Zoological Society to study the two species I missed at Cornell – the Black-necked Cranes of Tibet and the Siberian Cranes of Russia. Aware that a tiny population of Black-necked Cranes nested in northern India, and a small flock of Siberian Cranes wintered in India, I proposed a comprehensive study of Black-necked Cranes in spring and summer, and Siberian Cranes in autumn and winter. The proposal was approved. Unfortunately, a war between India and Pakistan forced me to change my plans. I transferred my studies to Japan and Australia where five crane species awaited my observations of displays in captivity compared to the same in the wild. Little did I know in 1971, that a major conservation challenge awaited me in Japan.

The autumn of 1971 witnessed the return of my *Cranium* cranes to their owners, the completion of the first draft of my thesis, and success with the oral exam. As scheduled, the *Cranium* was demolished and deposited in a landfill. The outdoor microphones at the Lab no longer transmitted the calls of cranes. I was off to Japan with a brief stop in Baraboo, Wisconsin to see Aldo Leopold's property and shack beside the river where he was inspired to write *Marshland Elegy*.

MY LIFE WITH CRANES

Cranes on the Farm

AN IDEA HATCHES

In Baraboo, Wisconsin, just a few miles from the abandoned farm where Aldo Leopold and his family helped "heal" the land, Ron Sauey was born in 1948, the year Leopold died fighting a spring wild fire. Ron's parents, Norman and Claire Sauey, were descendants of immigrants from Norway and Italy, respectively. Raised on a farm in northern Wisconsin, Norman received an eighth grade education. He was an intelligent, hard-working, and warm-hearted man. He was gentle yet determined – traits that led to great success in industry. On 65 acres on the north side of Baraboo, the Saueys built a beautiful home and facilities to accommodate a family of six and a herd of Arabian horses. But Wisconsin winters proved too severe for the valuable equines, and the Saueys and their herd eventually moved to a much larger property in Florida, leaving the farm buildings near Baraboo empty. They only returned for Christmas and summer.

Since childhood, Ron had a deep interest in nature, and like me, parents who understood and nurtured him. Also like me, he kept birds in captivity. He had several pheasant species that he maintained in a building with 12 fenced runs that later became the Chick House for our fledgling foundation. The nearby Leopold Reserve was a special place for Ron. He frequently went bird watching there with his high school biology teacher and mentor, Gerald Scott. Ron had a twin brother, Don, an older brother, Norman II, and a younger sister Mary Ann. The Sauey family was close-knit – Italian style. Ron's brothers, like their Dad, pursued careers in business. Ron was different. He was passionate about nature, to the consternation of his father. How would he make a living looking at birds and wildflowers?

During summer vacations from the University of Wisconsin, Ron tried working at the family plastics factory in Baraboo. Disturbed by the giant machines that exuded liquid plastic into molds and demanded three shifts every day to keep them producing continually, Ron knew that industry was not for him. He was cut from a different cloth. He preferred piano, cooking, and birding, while always maintaining a close relationship with his family and a small circle of intellectual friends that gathered during recesses in Gerald Scott's classroom.

VICTOR BAKHTIN

After completing a Bachelor's of Science degree in biology, Ron came to the Cornell Laboratory for Ornithology for graduate studies. The fall of 1971 marked Ron's first and my last semester at Cornell. It was an extremely busy time for me completing the first draft of my thesis, passing oral exams, returning cranes to their owners, and preparing for work in Japan. Although our offices were near each other, I had not met Ron until I overheard him telling someone he was from Wisconsin. I had a special interest in Wisconsin through Aldo Leopold and after introducing myself, I asked Ron if he knew about Leopold. I was amazed that Ron's home was just 10 miles from Leopold's shack beside the Wisconsin River, and that the Leopold Reserve was among his favorite birding spots. We always felt that Leopold introduced us!

A few weeks before I left Cornell, Ron and I volunteered to spend one Sunday afternoon helping with a census of the waterfowl of Lake Cayuga. The weather was too inclement to be outdoors so we opted for a warm restaurant in the countryside. That is where we shared a conversation that would change our lives forever. A magnificent pair of Wattled Cranes was the last to leave the *Cornell Cranium*. Ron had seen them through the perimeter fence and was impressed. He commented that it seemed a pity that my assemblage of cranes was dispersed just after the colony had been established and some pairs of cranes had started to breed. We agreed that a world center was needed for the conservation of cranes. Jokingly, I commented that cranes migrated across continents and a special branch of the United Nations was needed to coordinate conservation programs among politically polarized nations whose boundaries cranes could not recognize.

Ron told me about his family's empty horse farm in Baraboo. Ideas percolated. A few weeks later, just before Christmas on my way to Japan to

study Red-crowned Cranes, I spent several days with the Saueys and visited the Leopold shack. The Wisconsin winter and the open spaces with farms and forests reminded me of Nova Scotia, as did the warmth and kindness of the Sauey family, and Gerald and Gladys Scott. The big red horse barn on the Sauey property was relatively new and elegantly designed – fitting habitat for regal birds! Norman and Claire Sauey agreed to rent us the farm for $1.00 per year in order to create our Crane Branch of the United Nations. They were delighted that the abandoned farm would be used to create a career for their gifted son. The rent was just right, but it was the responsibility of the co-founders to raise support for operations.

During the following year while I worked first in Japan and then in Australia, through the generosity of his parents, Ron supervised the construction of 15 large aviaries on the Sauey farm. We exchanged extensive correspondence concerning the mission and goals of our crane center. We settled on a simple mission statement, *the mission of the International Crane Foundation is the study and preservation of cranes worldwide.* Five goals in order of priority included research, public education, habitat protection, captive breeding, and reintroduction.

A CLOSE CALL

In December of 1972, after a year in the field in Japan and Australia, it was time to return to Baraboo to begin my new life. After an 18-hour flight from Sydney to Chicago on December 22, heavy traffic and bad weather delayed our landing by a half-hour on that frigid and foggy winter evening. The last leg of my journey was to be a short 35-minute flight north from Chicago to Madison, Wisconsin. Upon arrival at the gate of the North Central Airlines flight to Madison, I was dismayed to discover I had missed the flight by 15 minutes. Ron would be waiting for me.

At that moment, I was so tired that it did not cross my mind to call the Madison Airport and page Ron. I drifted into a special reception area set up for soldiers returning from the Vietnam War and from a soft easy chair relished a cup of fresh coffee and a donut while watching TV. Suddenly, the program was interrupted for an emergency announcement. The North Central flight from Chicago to Madison had collided on takeoff with another airplane and there were heavy casualties. Stunned, I returned to the gate from which the flight had departed. On my way there, an announcement came, "Ladies and gentlemen, we are sorry to announce that due to the weather and field conditions, all flights from O'Hare International Airport are cancelled."

As dozens of planes unloaded and holiday travelers continued to arrive, the airport's expansive terminals were quickly filled by distressed customers. There was inadequate ground transportation to take the thousands of people from O'Hare to area hotels. People were stretched out on the floors. The restaurants ran out of supplies, as did the restrooms. The phone lines were overwhelmed and it was not until 3:00 a.m. that I finally got a call through to Ron assuring him that I had missed the ill-fated flight and that I was alive and well. The Sauey family had been up all night awaiting a call from the authorities that I was one of the 89 victims. The next day I arrived by bus and soon set up my temporary home in the lounge of the horse barn.

WHERE TO BEGIN?

Ron and I were very good friends, but we were also very different people. He was a cultured intellectual, brought up in affluence. I was raised in a big family near the wilderness of Nova Scotia, where hard physical work was stressed by both my parents and grandparents. I remember one hot day, my grandpa MacLeod took a bottle of water and a small boy (me) to the edge of a huge turnip field. He asked me to weed the whole patch row by row and then handed me the bottle of water. On another occasion, after Grandpa killed a bunch of chickens and thousands of feathers blew all across the barnyard, Grandma handed me a large paper bag and asked me to collect all the feathers. Every summer Mom would put on her old clothes and spend hours with us berry picking in patches of wild strawberries, raspberries, blueberries, and cranberries and say, "Stick to your bush, kids!" Scottish ethics were the norm – work hard, spend little!

During those early years in Baraboo, metaphorically speaking, I was facing weeds and feathers flying everywhere. Ron was not interested in working with the captive cranes and supervising the volunteers. From his father, he understood the importance of singular leadership. Ron excelled at public relations, from giving public tours to entertaining VIPs, a vital gift because our operational funds were scarce.

We had plenty of enthusiasm and ideas, but we knew nothing about legally establishing and properly managing a non-profit organization. Through the help of a conservation-minded lawyer in Baraboo, Forrest Hartmann, ICF's registration as a non–profit organization was secured in 1973. Aware of the great differences between the co-founders, and the importance of sound fiscal management, for the next five years Forrest met with us weekly to discuss a diversity of topics, and when possible, to pay the bills. Forrest was vital to the growth of the organization during those difficult early years when all of our staff were volunteers. In 1978, the capable Joan Fordham joined ICF and for the next 11 years provided sound administration through a period of rapid growth.

There was an old white farmhouse on the Sauey property. During those early years, that is where we all lived, including many volunteers. Ron spent much of his time at the adjacent estate of his parents. The Pierce family owned and operated a grocery store in Baraboo. Thanks to their generosity, we had a charge account. I purchased inexpensive, but wholesome food and filled the refrigerator at the White House. Sometimes our store debt exceeded $800. The meager donations that came from tours and speaking engagements paid the Pierces and the farmer's cooperative where we bought poultry food for the cranes.

In 1975, I moved from the White House to a two-room cabin in the forest two miles from ICF. My landlady, Eleanor Parson, lived next door in a lovely home. Having moved to the Baraboo Hills from the Chicago area, Mr. and Mrs. Parson lived in the cabin while their big house was being built. Unfortunately, Mr. Parson passed away, leaving his wife alone in the woods. Mrs. Parson, appropriately nicknamed Twinkle, often stopped by to see the cranes. We became lifelong friends and she invited me to live rent-free in the cabin. She even prepared my evening meals at her home, and we shared many evenings reading and playing Scrabble. The cabin also became a home for the volunteers. I don't know how we managed, but sometimes as many as seven of us inhabited those two rooms. I would prepare breakfast for everyone before they departed for ICF, leaving me to work peacefully at my desk in the back corner. The two small offices at ICF were already overcrowded especially in winter when the crane keepers came in from the cold.

In 1981, I married a lovely Japanese lady, Kyoko, who had volunteered at ICF the previous year. We shared the cabin for five years before buying an old farmhouse and 16 acres. The Parson family later gave the land, cabin, and Twinkle's house to ICF, the sale of which contributed to the growth of our budding endowment fund.

UNLOCKING THE SECRETS OF CRANE BEHAVIOR

When I worked as a bird keeper and crane researcher at the Alberta Game Farm during the summers of 1966 and 1967, the Director Al Oeming mentioned on several occasions that the enormous black and white Manchurian Cranes of East Asia (now called Red-crowned Cranes), dwarfed all other cranes in their magnificence. Throughout the ages, these cranes have been depicted in art and folklore as symbols of good luck, long life, happiness, and marital fidelity.

In the late 1960s, there were only two pairs of Red-crowned Cranes in captivity in the U.S. During my graduate research, I observed the pair in Pennsylvania. They lived in a large, rocky pasture shared with goats and donkeys. I broadcast recorded unison calls of wild Red-crowned Cranes near their enclosure. The two captive cranes suddenly became alert and each bird walked to adjacent mounds of earth beside a ditch along the far side of the pasture. With the bright red patch of bare skin expanding down over the back of their heads, and their bodies held rigid in threat posture, the cranes emitted a trumpet-like territorial duet, the one and only unison call. Instantly, this "pair" was identified as two males!

After they finished calling and with wings tightly closed, the cranes elevated their wings vertically above their backs while bending forward toward each other and rotating their heads sideways to contract their crimson crowns against a backdrop of black and white. During my observations of twelve other species of cranes, I had never seen such a spectacular display. I named it the Arch Threat Display. It appeared that the two male cranes were threatening each other. In just a few seconds, they had revealed something that was unique and fabulous. I felt like I had discovered a hidden treasure.

I traveled to Japan to study Red-crowned Cranes in the wild after completing my studies at Cornell. On the way, I stopped in Honolulu to see the other pair of Red-crowned Cranes. To my amazement and delight, as revealed by my new unison call sexing method, I immediately identified them as two females. I explained to the zoo director, Jack Thorpe, that there was another mismatched pair in Pennsylvania, and that the only two pairs in North American zoos had no hope of ever producing offspring. I also explained that by the time I came back from my overseas fieldwork in two years, there would be a newly formed center specifically for cranes in Baraboo, Wisconsin. Would he send the two females to Baraboo to pair with the two males from Pennsylvania? As usual, I had my fingers crossed that I could secure the males on loan and that everything would work out.

And it did.

When I returned from Japan and Australia to Baraboo in December of 1973, the four Red-crowned Cranes had arrived in Wisconsin – 2 females from Hawaii and 2 males from Massachusetts. One of the males and one of the females were feather perfect. Placing them side by side in a divided pen, I hoped that love would blossom. They immediately started unison calling together and I was thrilled. Some weeks later, they were finally placed together in the same pen under supervision. They walked side by side, danced, performed the unison call, and seemed compatible. Eventually, they were allowed together without supervision. One morning when I came to feed them, to my horror, I discovered the male had killed the female. Two months later the male died from liver cancer. The disease had likely changed his behavior based on his unexpected aggression toward his mate. I recalled the wisdom of my beloved mother, "George," she would say, "When you have livestock, you are also going to have deadstock!"

The other pair of Red-crowned Cranes had serious physical handicaps. The right wing of the male was detached from its socket and dangled around his leg. The female was so old and arthritic she could barely walk and could not crouch. They were unable to perform natural copulation due to their physical limitations, but that spring, the elderly female laid two eggs. Unable to crouch fully to lay her eggs, she awkwardly squatted above the nest and each fragile egg had a distance to travel before landing in the nest. Observing this unusual situation, I added a deep bed of straw to her nest, and henceforth each new egg gently bounced home.

The following spring, I collected semen from the male and artificially inseminated the female, producing ICF's first captive-produced crane chicks, Tancho and Tsuru (Japanese words for Red-crowned and crane). At one month, Tancho died, but Tsuru flourished and until he moved to our new site in 1981, delighted me with a daily flight in the sky over ICF. One day he joined a flock of migrating Tundra Swans and I thought we would lose him, but after a short time at the end of their "V" he broke ranks and returned for breakfast. His parents produced many offspring in subsequent years that we distributed to zoos. More Red-crowned Cranes were brought in from zoos in Europe and Japan, and soon there was a healthy captive population of these magnificent cranes in the U.S. Tsuru, who hatched in 1975, survives as one of the best breeders and one of the most aggressive cranes at ICF.

MY LIFE WITH CRANES

AN EPIDEMIC ERUPTS

The captive population at ICF bloomed to the point that during the winter of 1977-78, a ten-acre, securely fenced field was home to a flock of about 60 cranes of seven species. That spring I returned to Baraboo in mid-March from field work in Afghanistan. It was one of those mild balmy days. When I first walked into the field with the assortment of cranes, a juvenile Blue Crane walked up to me and collapsed. I noticed several other cranes looked ill. I was witnessing the beginnings of a disease outbreak. During the weeks that followed, 25 sick cranes had to be tube fed every few hours throughout the day and night. Only three survived. The chick house where many of the ill birds had been reared became the hospital where most of them perished. For the first time in my life, I was exhausted and somewhat psychologically paralyzed. Twenty-two cranes died from a formerly unknown disease that attacks the liver and spleen.

With assistance from the University of Wisconsin and the National Wildlife Health Laboratory in nearby Madison, the disease was eventually identified as a type of herpes virus that was subsequently named Inclusion Body

Disease in Cranes (IBDC). A test for the virus was developed, and 60 more cranes tested positive for IBDC including a pair of Hooded Cranes imported from a zoo several years before the outbreak. By testing serum collected annually by the Wildlife Health Lab from all cranes at ICF since 1973, that pair of Hooded Cranes were the only birds in the serum bank with a titer for IBDC. They had not been noticeably affected by the virus. However, their enclosure was adjacent to the field of the mixed flock. Apparently, the virus had somehow been transmitted to species that lacked resistance to the pathogen. Our "clean cranes" were concentrated in enclosures on the north side of the property separated by a field and a bit of forest from the "contaminated" cranes on the south side. Fortunately, our most valuable birds, the Whooping Crane, Tex, and the Siberian Cranes were among the safe group. To help maintain isolation, separate staff cared for each group of cranes. The outbreak at ICF resulted in an important medical discovery. Testing for IBDC has now become standard procedure in the management of both wild and captive cranes.

NEW BEGINNINGS

By the end of the outbreak, I was discouraged and tired. Our flock was reduced by more than 60 percent, our site was contaminated, our funds were scarce, and most of the staff were volunteers. How was ICF to survive?

The Secretary of the Smithsonian Institution in 1978, Dr. S. Dillon Ripley, was a renowned ornithologist and aviculturist. We met when he had served on the Board of Directors of the Cornell Laboratory for Ornithology while I was graduate student. He enjoyed observing my captive cranes in the *Cornell Cranium*. In the summer of 1978, after the dust settled from the outbreak, I called Dr. Ripley for advice about the future direction for ICF.

With his typical flare for optimism and bright ideas, Dr. Ripley encouraged me to contact all the people who had made a substantial financial contribution to ICF and to invite them to join the Board of Directors. Within two weeks, 18 major supporters met with Ron and me. Sixteen of them joined the Board. Mary Wickhem, an outstanding citizen from Janesville, Wisconsin, chaired that meeting and every other meeting of the Board, four

MY LIFE WITH CRANES

times a year, for the next 22 years. Everyone agreed that finding a new permanent home for ICF was a top priority.

The following winter while I worked in Korea, Mary and John Wickhem along with Ron Sauey inspected a 180-acre property a few miles north of the Sauey farm. As they pushed to the crest of a hill that bordered a deep glacial kettle on their cross-country skis, Ron noticed the seed heads of prairie plants poking up through the snow. The hill was covered by virgin prairie apparently spared from the plow because of the steep slope and sandy soil. Habitat restoration was one of our great interests for ICF. This property had the potential for conserving virgin prairie and for converting agricultural fields back to prairie. The property owner was ready to sell and ICF was ready to

buy. Just one year after an epidemic threatened to destroy ICF, our new Board of Directors met in 1979, and unanimously voted to buy the new property. From the ashes of tragedy arose a new, clean ICF supported by an enthusiastic and gifted Board of Directors and a reasonably paid staff under the guidance of a capable administrator Joan Fordham.

Ted Thousand

Dances with Whoopers

STUDYING WHOOPING CRANES AT PATUXENT

Often when I'm introduced at a speaking engagement, the story about my dance with Tex, the human-imprinted Whooping Crane, is recounted. I sometimes feel the audience expects me to dance up to the podium! It is a story shared with 22 million viewers when I appeared on the Johnny Carson Show in 1982, and it's been retold in many publications to people of all ages. But my work with Tex is only a small part of my involvement with these rarest of cranes.

My adventure with Whooping Cranes began in May of 1954 in a one-room schoolhouse in Stillwater, Nova Scotia – eight years old and the only student in the third grade. The formerly unknown nesting grounds of the Whooping Cranes in northern Canada had recently been discovered, and a dramatization about a pair of Whooping Cranes was broadcast on the weekly radio program, *Science of the Air*. The pair described the dangers along their 3,000-mile migration from wintering grounds in Texas, and finally their relief to reach an enormous impenetrable wetland complex – a place unknown to humans. Suddenly the sound of a low-flying aircraft was followed by the cries of the female crane, "Help, help! They found us. Now we will be shot, stuffed, and placed in a museum." The male crane comforted her, "No dear, this a safe place inside Wood Buffalo National Park. The Wood Bison survived here and so will we!"

The broadcast had a profound effect on me. From that point forward, I was deeply concerned about the welfare of Whooping Cranes. The radio broadcast also demonstrated the power of effective education in shaping the opinions of youngsters.

That was the beginning of my fascination with the welfare of our continent's tallest bird and one of the rarest species on the planet. The migratory flock had been reduced to just 16 individuals in 1942. In 1954, there were 24, and by 1966 when the governments of Canada and the United States first collected eggs from wild nests to establish a captive flock, there were about 44 birds.

In 1966, when I was an undergraduate student at Dalhousie University in eastern Canada and was employed by the Alberta Game Farm near Edmonton some 300 miles south of the nesting area of the Whooping Cranes, I had my first experiences with cranes in the wild as the calls of migrating Sandhill Cranes floated down from the skies. I was amazed that such a loud sound was produced by specks so high in the sky. I was also fascinated by reports in the news about the historic lift of Whooping Cranes eggs from the wild nests. The eggs were transported in a portable incubator across the continent to the Patuxent Wildlife Research Center in Maryland where they were hatched and the chicks were reared to start a captive flock. I would never have believed at the time that three years later, as a graduate student at Cornell University, I would be recording the behavior of Whooping Cranes at Patuxent. That is where I first met Tex.

TEX AND ME

Beginning in 1966, the Whooping Cranes at Patuxent were raised from eggs collected from nests of wild cranes. Whooping Cranes typically lay two eggs per clutch, but usually only rear one chick. Removing one egg from each nest and hatching the eggs in incubators did not harm productivity in the wild, and established a captive flock as a safeguard against extinction. There were about 15 cranes at Patuxent that year. Most of them were in a large fenced field where it was hoped that pairs would form. Another enclosure contained two cranes. A male named Canus, taken from the wild following a wing injury, and Tex, a female. While other cranes were somewhat afraid of humans, Tex was just the opposite. Whenever someone approached her enclosure, if she liked the way they looked, she approached and often danced. I returned to Patuxent several times during my three years at Cornell to study the Whooping Cranes. Tex appeared to have zero interest in Canus, but a great interest in humans.

Tex's father, Crip, was a juvenile Whooping Crane migrating south across Nebraska when one of his wings was broken. He was captured and eventually ended up at the San Antonio Zoo, where some years later he paired with an injured female crane named Rosie. They became an excellent breeding pair, produced many eggs and chicks, but unfortunately none of the young cranes survived, until the arrival of Tex in 1966. Wanting to protect her, the zoo director took Tex from her parents and raised her in his home for three weeks before sending her to Patuxent.

Unfortunately, such exposure exclusively to humans during her early life irreversibly imprinted Tex on our species. During the next decade, all efforts to pair Tex with a male Whooping Crane failed. Tex never laid an egg at Patuxent. When Crip and Rosie produced Tex in 1966, there were only 44 of their kind alive in the wild flock. Although the pair lived for many years after Tex hatched, they never produced more offspring. Tex was the sole recipient of their valuable genes.

I reasoned that if Tex had a human companion during the spring breeding season, she might be stimulated to ovulate and lay an egg. With the help of my Cornell colleague Dr. Cam Kepler, we convinced the powers-that-be to send Tex to the International Crane Foundation with the understanding that I personally would attempt to bring her into egg production. The summer of 1976 was the beginning of a seven-year saga that ended with the production of a single chick named Gee Whiz, the historic hatch that occurred just three weeks before Tex was killed by a pack of raccoons.

In Baraboo, Tex's home was a 15 x 15 x 7 foot wooden, unheated shelter, adjoining a 60 x 40 x 7 foot outdoor enclosure. During the summer of 1976, the indoor shelter was subdivided by chicken wire to provide an office and sleeping space for me, with Tex on the adjoining side with food, water and a door to her outside pen. From the start, Tex liked me. We often did the courtship dance, and while I worked at my desk she stood nearby preening. When she wanted me to follow her, she elevated her beak, faced in the direction she wanted to move, and emitted a soft purr. I followed her and the walk often turned into a dance.

Crane dancing kept me in shape – it was *Texercise!* The motions included bowing, jumping, running, and tossing small sticks in the air. The vigorous sequence usually lasted several minutes. By late summer, I moved back to my home, but visited Tex as time allowed. Separation did not seem to stress her. She always wanted to dance. From mid-March through late May of 1977, I spent all my daylight hours with Tex and continued with office work between dances. She finally came into breeding condition and laid a single egg. But the egg was slightly deformed with wrinkles on the pointed end. Of course, it was infertile as there was no male Whooping Crane at ICF at that time from which to collect semen and perform artificial insemination. But I had guessed correctly and we proved that she could lay an egg.

The Audubon Park Zoo in New Orleans agreed to send two males on breeding loan to ICF. We named them Tony and Angus. Tony was a poor specimen with a broken beak, crooked toes, unkempt plumage, a raspy strange voice, and an aggressive personality. He was never a viable donor for Tex. Angus was feather perfect, an excellent semen producer, and mild mannered. In 1978, through artificial insemination, Tex produced a single fertile egg! Unfortunately, the chick died while hatching. Not long after that, Angus perished from injuries sustained as he flew into the side of his enclosure when a hot air balloon that floated overhead frightened him. His death was an enormous loss for us.

MY LIFE WITH CRANES

In 1979, I again worked with Tex, but she laid only one soft-shelled egg that broke. In 1980, because I was away, a colleague, Yoshimitzu Shigeta, tried to work with Tex, but she disliked him and never laid an egg. In 1981, our Curator of Birds, Mike Putnam, danced with Tex as time allowed. She came into breeding condition but still never laid an egg. Finally in 1982, before moving to our new site six miles away, I decided to make an all-out effort to get a chick from Tex.

I built a 6 x 4 x 5 foot shed, moved it to the crest of a hill in a hayfield adjacent to Tex's enclosure, and equipped the shed with a desk, chair, manual typewriter, battery-operated radio, sleeping bag and a shovel for lavatory needs. The staff affectionately referred to my little shed as the "love shack." That was my home from late March through May. Writing and office work kept me occupied much of the day, broken only by walks and dances with Tex, and mail delivery at noon by our administrator Joan Fordham. When people entered our field, Tex became defensive and wanted to attack them. In contrast, when wild Sandhill Cranes flew over or landed nearby, Tex ignored them.

When I didn't appear in church for several Sundays, my pastor was concerned and thought perhaps I was "losing it." Tex disliked many people, but she especially despised women and people with red hair! Unfortunately, the pastor qualified in the latter category, but he was a man of faith so he ignored Tex's threat displays, and calmly sat on the grass in our territory.

While we chatted and I assured him that the ordeal with Tex was building my faith, Tex came up behind him and delivered a hard peck to the back of his cranium. The poor man reeled and soon departed. On another occasion, I was alarmed to see Tex chasing a tail-raised skunk. When I called her name, she stopped abruptly and started her part of the unison call as the skunk ran away. I had narrowly escaped living with a very smelly Whooping Crane.

During this time, fresh Whooping Crane semen was sent from Patuxent in Maryland twice weekly and administered to Tex. In late May, Tex laid an egg! We immediately placed it under a pair of reliable captive Sandhills, and I remained with Tex night and day hoping for a second egg. Our routine was quite amusing. Tex's nest containing a dummy egg was beside my shed. It is the duty of members of a crane pair to alternate incubation responsibilities. After incubating for several hours, Tex would leave the nest to forage for earthworms in our field. I would then place my folded sleeping bag over the nest, over which I placed my little table and chair. After some time, when she returned, I moved my materials back into the shed, and she resumed incubation.

It was the night of May 25, 1982. Total darkness, deluges of rain, flashing lightning, crashing thunder, and within a few feet of my tiny shed on the grassy hilltop, the soft purr of a very wet human-imprinted Whooping Crane named Tex. From my comfortable sleeping bag behind a small wooden door,

MY LIFE WITH CRANES

I spoke words I hoped would bring her comfort as she faithfully incubated a dummy egg. She answered with more purrs. But when warnings of tornados were announced over the radio, I decided we had reached a breaking point. Abandoning hope that Tex might lay a second egg, I emerged from my shelter and picked up the huge bird that I had courted from dawn till dark over the last seven weeks. Her nest was saturated and so was she. She did not resist me cradling her with legs folded in incubation posture, as I made my way down the hill to her permanent residence. Unable to hold both a flashlight and a crane, we continued in the darkness and the ferocity of the elements. When I spoke, she answered. She never struggled, and I sensed that she felt safe. Soon she was secure in her dry home. I cherish that memory of such a unique connection between man and bird.

Unfortunately, there was no second egg. After two weeks, Tex's egg was taken from the sandhills and brought to a dark room that contained a box with a bright light inside and a small round opening. By holding the egg against the hole, the bright light lit up the contents of the egg. There was a chick developing. Hooray! However, as with Tex's other eggs, there were problems.

The pointed end was wrinkled and the egg was losing weight so rapidly that the survival of the chick was threatened. After consulting with Dr. Bernard Wentworth at the Department of Poultry Science at the University of Wisconsin, we were encouraged to hydrate the egg by submerging it for 10 minutes in ice water. The temperature drop would cause  contraction of the liquid contents in the egg. Atmospheric pressure on the water would then force water into the vacuum. It worked. The egg gained weight and hatched with a helping hand from Mike Putnam.

But the new chick was underweight and incapable of swallowing water and food. It appeared that dehydration was causing constriction of the esophagus. Despite subcutaneous injections of fluids, the chick continued to lose weight. Finally, we were forced to gently thread a tiny tube down the chick's esophagus to inject food. The chick's health rapidly improved and soon was eating and drinking. We named him Gee Whiz, after Dr. George Gee from the Patuxent who collected and sent the semen.

To assure that he imprinted on cranes, Gee Whiz was raised with a group of Red-crowned Crane chicks. Gee Whiz lived with a female Red-crowned Crane until 1989 when the flock of Whooping Cranes at Patuxent was divided and 22 birds were sent to the International Crane Foundation. He subsequently paired with a female Whooping Crane named Ooblek, and they have produced many offspring to contribute both to the captive flock and to release efforts to establish new wild flocks.

In 1990, I joined the 10-person International Whooping Crane Recovery Team (Canada-USA), and I continue in that role to help guide research and conservation programs for the only self-sustaining wild population, and to help with captive management and release programs. It has been a rewarding experience to promote public interest in the wild Whooping Cranes on their Texas wintering grounds, through a Whooping Crane Festival convened in late February annually in Port Aransas since 1996.

A few years ago, one of my greatest pleasures was to visit a pair of reintroduced wild Whooping Cranes nesting in a wetland on a cranberry farm about 60 miles north of Baraboo, Wisconsin. The female of this pair was an offspring of Gee Whiz – so I fondly thought of her as my "daughter." For several years, the pair only produced infertile eggs, but eventually, a researcher checking on their nest was thrilled to be greeted by a chick in the nest – my granddaughter! It brings me great satisfaction that our efforts with Tex proved successful, and I consider it symbolic for most of our programs that require many years of patience, perseverance, and faith before the tide turns in favor of conservation.

JOHN WRIGHT

Red-Crowned Cranes

WINTER IN HOKKAIDO

Standing five feet tall with a red crown, bright white plumage and contrasting black neck and inner wing feathers, the Red-crowned Crane has always been a treasure both in nature and in zoos. During my graduate days, I was thrilled to study the only representatives of this species on the mainland of North America – two elderly males. In 1971, when I completed my work at Cornell, I wanted to study Red-crowned Cranes in the wild in East Asia. China was in the midst of the Cultural Revolution. My letters to Chinese ornithologists were not answered. China, with its eight crane species, was closed to outsiders. Consequently, my attention focused on a small population of Red-crowned Cranes that lived in the far north of Japan on the island of Hokkaido.

Until the 1800s, Japan was a feudalistic country in which cranes were protected by the ruling classes. After Emperor Meiji abolished many of the ancient laws and opened Japan's doors to the outside world, the cranes lost their special status. Wetlands where cranes lived were drained to create farmland. Red-crowned Cranes that nested in northern areas on the island of Honshu and throughout Hokkaido were hunted ruthlessly. By the turn of that century, they were believed to be extirpated from Japan.

Southeastern Hokkaido with its enormous wetlands became the last frontier for wilderness and the last refuge for the indigenous Ainu people. In 1924, a team of scientists on an ornithological expedition to southeastern Hokkaido

Senshu University in Bibai

Kushiro Marsh (Kushiro-Shitsugen National Park, Hokkaido)

JAPAN

★ TOKYO

Dorn Moore

discovered a tiny population of perhaps 30-50 Red-crowned Cranes. They had escaped persecution by not migrating and by the protection of the Ainu as "Marsh Gods." In spring and summer, they nested and reared their young on the huge, pie-shaped Kushiro Marsh and on coastal wetlands. During the winter when these wetlands were locked in ice, the cranes frequented areas of open water at hot springs and along brooks and rivers. Eventually the cranes and the central portion of the Kushiro Marsh were protected by the Government of Japan's Ministry of Education as Natural Monuments and their population remained small but stable.

The winter of 1952 was unusually cold, and many of the springs and streams where the cranes fed on fish, invertebrates, and plants were frozen. Local people noticed the plight of the cranes, and not knowing what else to do, they scattered corn on the snow. The cranes accepted the handout and the tradition of feeding the cranes was born. As several major crane-feeding stations were established on the pastures of farms, the numbers of cranes steadily increased through the next decade and then leveled off at about 170 birds.

In the early 1960s, the Japanese Broadcasting Company created an impressive film entitled, *Red-crowned Cranes in Four Seasons*. The producer of that film, Reiji Nakatsubo, gave me a copy of the film while I was at

MY LIFE WITH CRANES

Cornell. The film contained spectacular footage of wild Red-crowned Cranes dancing on the snow and performing their arch threat displays and unison calls. Eager to check the behavior of cranes in the wild against behavior that I had recorded from captive birds, I decided that Hokkaido was a destination where cranes could easily be observed in winter at the feeding stations. In February 1972, I began a remarkable adventure in Japan that later culminated at the Imperial Palace.

A handsome and exceptionally quiet man, Professor Hiroyuki Masatomi is the world's leading expert on the Red-crowned Crane. Over the past fifty years, he has published prolifically on the cranes. He had a home beside the Kushiro Marsh and together with a corps of students and volunteers was a driving force in crane research and conservation. Dr. Masatomi's close friends were the four members of the Satsuki family in the city of Kushiro near the Kushiro Marsh. Dr. Satsuki, an obstetrician, was a jovial intellect with keen interests in medicine, philosophy, languages, anthropology, music, natural

Hiroyuki Masatomi

VICTOR BAKHTIN

history, photography, and conservation. Mrs. Satsuki was the bookkeeper and the administrator of her husband's small hospital. They had two gifted daughters, Yulia and Rori – both accomplished violinists and fluent in English. Dr. Masatomi and the Satsukis were to be my great friends and helpers in Hokkaido.

When I arrived in Hokkaido, Dr. Masatomi was recovering from injuries sustained in a serious car accident. We met briefly at his office at Senshu University in Bibai, about five hours northwest of Kushiro by train. He suggested that I ask for help with logistics from the Satsuki family in Kushiro, as the crane feeding stations in the countryside were far from hotels and restaurants. I felt like a newborn without language in a foreign but very friendly culture. By the time my train pulled into Kushiro, it was dark, snowing, and the wind was blowing. I will never forget the memory of the smiling face framed by snow-covered hair at the train door– it was Dr. Satsuki. "You must be George Archibald. Come quickly. My family and friend await you."

A kind and humorous graduate student, Tamaki Kitagawa, was studying the Red-crowned Cranes. He lived in a tent in an abandoned thatch-roofed farmhouse a few miles from the crane feeding station at the farm of Mr. and Mrs. Watanabe near the village of Tsuru (Crane Village). That first evening in Kushiro, Dr. Satsuki introduced me to Tamaki and Tamaki invited me to join him in the field. For the rest of the winter and into spring, Tamaki's tent was my home too. He introduced me to the intricacies of the lives of the Red-crowned Cranes. In the natural world, few scenes can compare to the spectacle of Red-crowned Cranes in blue winter skies on snow-covered landscapes with a backdrop of gray forests, frozen wetlands, and smoldering volcanoes. It was a privilege to live so near the cranes and it was a thrill to study the complex communication system within their society. But man, was it cold!

In winter, most of the cranes in Hokkaido gather in flocks at the feeding stations during the day, and at night, they roost in the shallow water of nearby streams. From the Watanabe's yard and along the riverbanks, we watched the cranes from dawn until dark and then returned to the tent. I wore several layers of warm clothing topped by a thick snowmobile suit. Our food consisted of boiled noodles, nuts, and biscuits followed by a small glass of whiskey to open our pores and evoke an impression of comfort. Fatigued by a day in the field, wearing snowmobile suits in our sleeping bags, we always instantly fell asleep. To my delight, I was toasty warm upon waking and ready for more noodles. Weight was not gained that winter and Dr. and Mrs. Satsuki worried that winter camping would not benefit our health. We were often abruptly summoned by telephone to their home. It was an extremely cold drive by motorbike the 18 miles to Kushiro, but soon we were warm, bathed, fed, and benefiting from the inspirational company of the Satsukis and their guests.

MARSH GODS

Within the flocks of cranes, there are mated pairs, pairs with one or two juveniles, and unpaired adult-plumaged birds in groups of varying sizes. At the time of fledging in late summer, the plumage of the juveniles is predominantly brown. During the autumn and winter, the brown feathers are gradually replaced by white feathers. Each juvenile is at a slightly

MY LIFE WITH CRANES

International Crane Foundation
E 11376 Shady Lane Rd.
Baraboo
WI 53913
Tel: 1-608-356-9462
savingcranes.org
shop@savingcranes.org

Date: 5/1/2021 1:01:05 PM
INVOICE No: 1-72204
Cashier BevP

Description Qty	Price	Ext. Price

My Life with Cranes
| 1723 | 1 @ $19.95 | $19.95 |
| -Discount 10% | ($2.00) | $17.96T |

	Sub Total:	$17.96
	Tax1:	$0.98
	Total:	$18.94

| Tendered: | | $18.94 |
| Visa: | | $18.94 |
Card #: ***********4995
Element TransID: 1176625979

---

* YOUR TOTAL SAVINGS: $2.00 *

International Crane Foundation
E 11376 Shady Lane Rd.
Baraboo
WI 539.3
Tel: 1-608-356-9462
savingcranes.org
shop@savingcranes.org

Date: 5/1/2021 1:01:05 PM
INVOICE No:
Cashier: 204

Description Qty Price Exc.Price

My Life with Cranes
...1723   1 @ $19.95 $19.95
-Discount 10% ($2.00) $17.95

Sub Total: $17.95
Tax: $0.98

Total: $18.94

Tendered:
Visa: $18.94
Card #: ***********4995
Element TransID: 117665252?9

* YOUR TOTAL SAVINGS: $2.00 *

different stage in the molt and can therefore be individually recognized. The juveniles stay close to their parents through winter. Tamaki and I identified all of the chicks and therefore each of the family groups at the feeding station.

The Japanese knew that the Kushiro Marsh and the wetlands in eastern Hokkaido were nesting areas for several pairs of cranes. However, as the population increased to about 170 birds, it was assumed that most of the birds migrated to Siberia in spring to breed. They knew and loved the cranes in winter at the feeding stations, but for the rest of the year the cranes were out of sight and out of mind. Believing that most of the cranes would migrate to Russia in late winter, I planned to return to Wisconsin in April.

In March, as the days became a bit warmer and significantly longer, the cranes danced more and many pairs started to mate. Gradually, the numbers of cranes at the feeding station declined as the pairs migrated back to their breeding grounds. Juvenile cranes usually migrate with their parents, so when the juveniles continued to come to the feeding station without their parents, I reasoned that the adults had not actually migrated to Russia but were breeding somewhere in Japan.

Dr. Satsuki had been informed that most of the wetlands in southeastern Hokkaido were zoned lowlands for reclamation amenable to farming, a scarcity in Japan. Supported and encouraged by her father, Yulia Satsuki visited many municipal offices within the distribution of the cranes and confirmed that most of the wetlands were doomed. There was also another serious problem. Near the feeding stations, many cranes were killed by colliding with power lines. For a decade the population had not increased. Death by collision seemed to be the major limiting factor to growth, a problem that could be corrected by attaching bright markers to the lines.

If most of the cranes migrated to Siberia to breed and then returned to Japan in autumn to spend the winter at the feeding stations, the population could possibly be maintained even if the wetlands in Hokkaido were destroyed. However, if the majority of the cranes nested on Japanese soil as I was beginning to suspect, the population would certainly decline due to the loss of nesting habitat. The failure of the young cranes to migrate led me to conclude that perhaps their parents were breeding in Japan – but where? Equipped only with a motorbike and a tent, how could Tamaki and I prove that most of the cranes were nesting in Japan? There were no roads to the wetlands where cranes might be nesting, and the forests that bordered the wetlands were rife with millions of disease-carrying ticks and a few dangerous bears.

In April, we surveyed the Kushiro Marsh from nearby hills. Distant unison calls floating up from locations in the impassible wetland indicated the probable location of a breeding pair. But it was almost impossible to observe the cranes, let alone see their nests. How could we conclusively prove that all the wetlands of southeastern Hokkaido were occupied by nesting cranes? By mid-May, the frustration was mounting as Yulia gathered more information about the plans for land reclamation. Tamaki and I could hear more and more pairs calling from unprotected Japanese wetlands. I had observed first-hand wetland destruction around much of the Kushiro Marsh.

One sunny morning in mid-May after breakfast with the Satsukis, I took Tamaki's motorbike along a dirt road that topped a dike into the heart of the Kushiro Marsh. I stopped where the Kushiro River first met the road and gazed out over that ocean of dried grasses from the previous year. As I contemplated the fate of the wetlands and the demise of the cranes, I heard the distant staccato of a helicopter. It appeared over the eastern hills and descended in my direction. It hovered briefly over the center of the wetland and then continued on to the west. This was the first time I had ever observed a helicopter or any other small aircraft in this remote corner of Hokkaido. Suddenly the idea popped into my brain. We must make an aerial survey over the wetlands to search for crane nests! From the air, crane nests, especially those of white cranes, are easily seen as doughnut-shaped formations with a pile of vegetation in the center (upon which the incubating crane sits), surrounded by a ring of water bordered by tall reeds.

Soon Dr. Satsuki was on the telephone with Dr. Masatomi. A newspaper company in Sapporo agreed to provide $1,000 worth of flying time, if we could match their contribution. There was enough money left in my research grant. The next morning Masatomi, Tamaki, and I flew over the wetlands of southeastern Hokkaido and spotted 53 doughnuts each with an incubating crane over a 250-mile span east to west along the southeast coast of Hokkaido. The survey provided the proof that the cranes were resident in Japan and that many were nesting on small wetlands slated for destruction.

Fortified with a map showing the location of the nests and wetlands and a set of color slides showing cranes colliding with power lines, I spoke in Sapporo

at the annual meeting of the Nature Conservation Association of Hokkaido and then in Nara at the annual meeting of the Japan Nature Congress. The Satsukis and other colleagues arranged for me to meet with officials in Kushiro, Sapporo and Tokyo. The media went wild with the crane story. I was honored to meet Minister Ishi, the first leader of the newly created Ministry of the Environment. He promised to investigate the problems facing the cranes. But it wasn't all a bed of roses – there was some resentment of our work. In a society steeped in protocol, a reporter once asked me what right I had, as an outsider, to meddle in Japanese affairs. Impetuously, I responded

MY LIFE WITH CRANES

in English that it was attitudes like his that caused wars. Dr. Satsuki was shocked by my response and burst out to Yulia in English, "Don't translate that. He might kill the interpreter!"

Before leaving Japan, I met Japan's foremost ornithologist, the founder and director of the Yamashina Institute for Ornithology, Dr. Yoshimaro Yamashina, and the Founder and Director of the Wild Bird Society of Japan, Mr. Godo Nakanishi. Together we had a pleasant audience with the Crown Prince Akihito on a sunny and very hot afternoon in late July at the Akasaka Palace in the heart of Tokyo. We were thrilled when Japan's National Bird, the Japanese Green Pheasant, appeared on the lawn. Apparently, the Imperial complex surrounded by Tokyo harbored the last pure genetic line of these pheasants, others having been influenced by Ring-necked pheasants imported and released from mainland Asia.

The next year, the Ministry of Environment embarked on a study of the cranes in Hokkaido, and came to the same conclusions as Tamaki and I had. Subsequently, the power lines around the feeding stations were made more obvious to cranes by sliding bright yellow plastic pipe over the wires. The oil crisis of 1973 dampened the economy and plans to drain the wetlands were set aside. Some of the wetlands were protected, and in 1987, the core area of the Kushiro Marsh was proclaimed a National Park. After a decade with no population change, the cranes have responded by a steady increase to more than 1,850 birds in the winter of 2016.

The International Crane Foundation's first VIP visitor was Dr. Yamashina who spent a week with us in the summer of 1973. Yoshimitzu Shigeta and Kuni Momose, researchers from the Yamashina Institute, shared my cabin with me for six months in 1980 and studied the cranes at ICF. After returning to Japan, Kuni journeyed to Hokkaido to study the cranes. He met Yulia Satsuki and they were later married. Today Kuni and Yulia Momose lead a productive private organization in Kushiro, the Red-crowned Crane Conservancy. Dr. Masatomi retired from Senshu University, continues his crane research, and is now joined in the field by his son Yoshiyuki Masatomi.

After receiving his Master of Science degree on the biology of Red-crowned Cranes, Tamaki Kitagawa did a doctorate on crows, and then became a high school biology teacher. We kept in touch and sometimes met in Tokyo. Finally after retiring, he spent a year at ICF studying a diversity of topics. This experience was followed by a spring and summer at Muraviovka Park, Russia where he studied both Red-crowned and White-naped Cranes.

At the Yamashina Institute for Ornithology, Kuni worked with Princess Sayako, the Emperor's daughter and part-time student of birds. I met the Princess on several occasions and in 1995 invited her to visit the International Crane Foundation in Baraboo, Wisconsin. She came in 1996 with an entourage of 42 people including the Japanese Ambassador, the Consulate-General of Japan in Chicago, their wives, four ladies in waiting, and a squadron of bodyguards all aboard a chartered aircraft. To return our hospitality a year later, the Princess invited a major supporter of ICF and collector of Japanese art, Mary Burke, and me for an audience with her parents. Crown Prince Akihito, whom I met in 1972, was now the Emperor.

Unfortunately, my adopted Japanese parents, Dr. and Mrs. Satsuki have passed away. However, their kindness, humor, and unlimited generosity to a total stranger interested in the greater good, made a deep and lasting impression on me. They embodied and exemplified the power of love, as did my own parents. I often think of these special people when a visitor appears at ICF or a letter arrives from a stranger. My work with the wild cranes in Hokkaido and with the people of Japan in 1972 marked my baptism into the world of international research and conservation and created an abiding love for Japan and its people. Part of my spirit will always be with those gorgeous cranes that seem to dance more than other cranes.

A TOUCH OF CLASS
MARY JACKSON BURKE

The largest collection of Japanese art in the world outside of Japan, including many pieces depicting cranes, rested for several decades in Manhattan, New York, in the mini-museum of art collector and philanthropist, Mary Jackson Burke (1916-2012). Mary and I were close friends for 36 years. I am often asked how Mary and I became friends.

At a dinner party, Mary had heard that a new organization dedicated to the conservation of cranes existed in central Wisconsin. In 1976, I received a call from Mary. She had recently visited northern Japan, and was thrilled to experience Red-crowned Cranes. She soon chartered a flight and we met at ICF where at that time, we had accumulated approximately 100 cranes of 14 species.

The previous year ICF hosted the first gathering of what later became the North American Working Group on Cranes. Three crane specialists from Japan and about 60 specialists from North America gathered for several days to present research reports about cranes, reports that had been assembled into a volume for which support was needed to publish. Mary Burke's Foundation made that happen.

Several years later on the Platte River in Nebraska, at 5:00 a.m. on a cold March morning, we were escorted in the dark to a rectangular wooden building with windows on one side from which we could see the multitudes of cranes standing side by side in the shallows. Dressed in several layers of warm clothing, Mary peered into the darkness. There was not a breath of wind. The cranes were silent and sleeping, likely on one leg with head and neck tucked under their wings. We waited for light. As the first rays of sunshine bathed the dawn in red, a thin layer of fog appeared above the cranes. In small groups, cranes rose from the river, disappeared into the fog and reappeared as they climbed into the sky. I had never seen such a magnificent interplay of water, cranes, fog and soft light before. Mary was mesmerized as nature and art combined. She had just witnessed what Japanese artists had seen and painted since ancient times. Her scrolls came to life. Subsequently, in her lectures, Mary joyfully shared her remarkable experience with cranes in Nebraska.

A lover of nature since childhood, one of her favorite places was a hemlock forest in a moss-covered swampy area near the family summer home, *The Forest Lodge,* beside Lake Namakagon in northern Wisconsin. This was her fairyland. In an era when privileged young women were expected to marry and have children, Mary elected an advanced education in psychology at Sarah Lawrence and Columbia Universities. Mary and her husband, Jackson, had a keen interest in Japan and its art. As a thank you for hosting the visit of Princess Sayako, the daughter of the Emperor and Empress of Japan, I was invited to the Imperial Palace for an afternoon audience with the royals. When I informed the Imperial Household that Mary Burke was in Tokyo, they proposed that she join me for the visit. We were thrilled to be with these gracious people and to see their art treasures. It was a wonderful visit.

Eventually Mary's collection was honored by an exhibition in Tokyo's National Museum. The collection continued to grow and in 1987, Mary was awarded the highest honor by the Japanese Government, the Order of Sacred Treasure.

THE LAND OF
THE MORNING CALM

The Korean peninsula is both a migratory corridor and wintering area for three species of threatened cranes: Red-crowned Cranes, White-naped Cranes and Hooded Cranes wintering mainly in South Korea. In 1973, through a generous grant from the New York Zoological Society, the newly formed International Crane Foundation supported a biologist, Dr. Kim Hon Kyu, to survey cranes wintering in South Korea. He found Red-crowned and White-naped Cranes in and near the western portions of the 2.5-mile wide Demilitarized Zone (DMZ) that had separated the Koreas

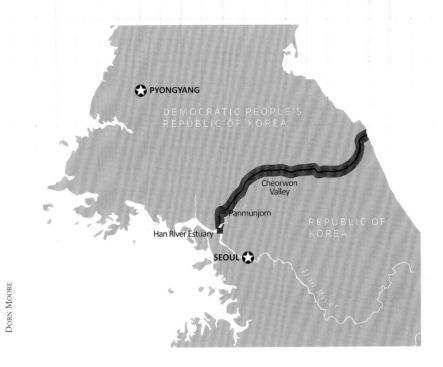

since the end of the Korean War in 1953. At that time, James Schlesinger was the U.S. Secretary of Defense, and approximately 78,000 U.S. soldiers were stationed in South Korea, many near the DMZ. I had heard that Schlesinger was a birder, so I wrote a letter to my friend Dr. S. Dillon Ripley, then the Secretary of the Smithsonian Institution, to see if he might inquire from Secretary Schlesinger whether I might have permission to study cranes in the southern portion of the DMZ where cranes had been spotted. It worked. In November of 1974, I was in the DMZ after signing an agreement that if I were killed or captured, the United Nations would deny any responsibility.

The 154-mile long DMZ is predominantly mountainous punctuated by river valleys and one wide basin, the Cheorwon Plain. In the west, three rivers, the Han, the Imjin, and the Sacheon flow respectively from the south, north, and east into a huge estuary that boasts the second highest tides in the world. In 1974, my work concentrated on the estuary of the Han River and the inland floodplain of the Sacheon River at Panmunjom – the famous place where officials from the two Koreas met, and where the 1953 Armistice was signed at the end of the Korean War.

From this estuary of the Han River, I looked north to the hills of North Korea. Security concerns associated with this open passageway from North Korea to Seoul resulted in heavy fortifications with land mines, high fences, guard posts, and an absence of people. Twice daily, the estuary fills and at low tide a wide expanse of grassland and mudflats is exposed – perfect feeding habitat for White-naped Cranes and thousands of Bean and White-fronted Geese. Several miles south of the border of the DMZ on the east side of the Han Estuary in a district called Munbali, a small peninsula juts out into the estuary. The peninsula is an outpost for the South Korean army. That is where I lived with the Korean soldiers during the month of November in 1974, and observed more than 1,000 White-naped Cranes foraging on the roots, seeds, and tubers of aquatic plants in the upper tidal zone.

At night, I shared an underground bunker measuring about 10x30 feet with 14 soldiers. Windowless but with a door opening to a stairwell at either end, a center corridor was bordered by a wide wooden platform where everyone slept side by side. A shelf along the far wall and above the platform provided a small storage place for the personal belongings of each soldier. A tiny wood stove with a pipe leading up through the ceiling and a single bare light bulb on the ceiling created habitat for the soldiers at night. The drop toilet was some distance away. Meals consisted of rice, kimchi (pickled cabbage), and pickled fish. This was home for each soldier for two years of compulsory military service.

I was certainly a novelty in the camp, and I was always treated with kindness and respect. My daylight hours were spent sitting on an old grave mound peering through my telescope and recording information on crane behavior. One evening was particularly memorable for me. A huge yellow sun was sinking low over the hills on the opposite side of the estuary. A wide expanse

of mud flats separated the grasslands of the upper tidal zone from the riverbed. Undoubtedly wishing to drink, a flock of White-naped Cranes left the grassland and literally danced across the slick mud to the river. I will never forget that special moment when the wetland, the dancing cranes, and the sunset all met as one. Much of the day, the flocks of cranes stood on the grasslands digging in the mud for food items. They seldom flew, and they also slept there at night. At high tide they walked in shallow water. Their survival depended on this fragile habitat inadvertently protected by warring nations in a region, which under normal conditions would have become a congested seaport.

One night we had a party in the bunker. One of the soldiers had completed his tenure with the army, and would depart for civilian life the following day. Dried fish slightly burned over our hot stove filled the room with smoke and a bad odor. Rice wine gladdened the heart but sickened my stomach. I had to escape to relieve myself. But, at night it was "shoot to kill" if a human was observed outside designated locations. I was in such discomfort that I took the risk, climbed the stairs, and in the darkness slowly crawled along a trench. Soon I felt better. Looking up, I was amazed at the brightness of the stars in the cold sky. There was not a breath of wind. Silence. Then suddenly the calls of a thousand cranes erupted from the nearby wetland. Something had alarmed them. The moment of glory evaporated quickly with the realization that perhaps their noise would alert the guards. Ever so slowly, I crawled back to the bunker.

The next morning, when our friend departed, he and several other soldiers wept openly. I was impressed that these seemingly macho men, who proudly walked barefoot across the snow and ice from the bunker to the toilet, were so uninhibited in expressing their feelings. Later, I was not surprised to learn that some Korean film actors were extremely popular in Japan because of their ability to express emotion.

While I was conducting my research at this camp, Professor Kim Hon Kyu, accompanied by an official from the Ministry of Culture and Information, visited me. Several months after I was able to show them such a remarkable assemblage of cranes, the South Korean government proclaimed the Han River Estuary a National Natural Monument.

I then moved northeast from the Han River Estuary to Panmunjom, where I was the guest of the United Nations Command for one month. I slept in a clean, cozy, heated room at Camp Kitty Hawk along the southern border of the DMZ. The camp was next to the only road leading to the international meeting place, Panmunjom, and from there into North Korea. The single gate through the southern fence opened to a two-lane paved road that traversed a section studded with land mines before entering the forested hills untouched by humans since the end of the war. A guard post sat atop a high hill in the center of a valley of rice paddies.

Every morning at 8:00 a.m., a line of vehicles carrying soldiers and officials covered the two miles from Camp Kitty Hawk to Panmunjom, and then returned at 4:00 p.m. My Korean bodyguard and I were always transported

MY LIFE WITH CRANES

to and from the DMZ on that schedule. I had eight hours to study about 40 Red-crowned and 100 White-naped Cranes that foraged in harvested fields. They were usually in the fields by the time we arrived and were still there when we left. Their roost area remained a mystery until one extremely cold morning when the cranes were absent. We climbed to a hilltop that provided a commanding view into an unexpected forested valley that contained a frozen reservoir. To our amazement and delight, all the cranes were standing on the ice at the far end of the reservoir. Cranes remain longer at their roost during cold weather to conserve energy. By late morning when it was warmer, and they were hungrier, they flew to the fields. We walked across the ice to the roost area and were amazed that the impressions of their legs were melted into the ice where some birds sat on the ice.

Typically, the cranes dispersed in small groups to many fields and wetlands to feed. One day, however, a bitterly cold wind moved in from the north. I took refuge in a rice straw hide I had built with a commanding view of North Korea and of a favorite feeding place for cranes. Family-by-family, and flock-by-flock, cranes of both species flew in from all directions and gathered on the field near my blind. The drastic drop in temperature and the winds stimulated them to flock together. I wondered if they might migrate further south. They did not.

A SURPRISING DISCOVERY IN THE DMZ

While the cranes were gathering, far across the valley in North Korea four egret-sized birds were also in flight. Several times previously, I had seen them at a great distance. But this time was different. They were flying toward the cranes – and me. In an instant, I had them in my 600 mm lens. As they approached, their white feathers turned to pale pink, their beaks elongated into long curved protrusions, and their red faces glistened in the cold air. I could scarcely believe my eyes. They were Crested Ibis! I was so shocked I was unable to snap the camera's shutter. Long thought to be extirpated from Korea, the Crested Ibis, *Daouge* in Korean, *Toki* in Japanese, are pale pink birds with salmon-yellow flight feathers,

orange-tipped beaks, orange legs, and bright red faces. They are without a doubt one of the most beautiful creatures of East Asia.

There is a sad Korean folk song about the *Daouge,* and the sound of the word in Korea mimics the plaintive call of the species that has suffered throughout its range in Japan, Korea, and China. Once a common bird throughout much of northeast Asia, the ibis lived in harmony with people. They frequently foraged in rice paddies and roosted and nested in nearby trees. Their salmon tail feathers adorned imperial swords in Japan.

I first became familiar with the story of the Crested Ibis when I was in graduate school at Cornell University and wrote a paper about the history of conservation in Japan. Although revered by the Japanese as a special Natural Monument, the ibis fell on hard times. Widespread hunting after the Meiji Restoration of 1867 when ibis were no longer protected by the ruling classes reduced their numbers. When wet rice paddies where the ibis foraged in winter were drained in autumn to reduce human diseases transmitted by snails, ibis numbers dropped. Toxic pesticides applied to crops after the Second World War further affected their numbers. When I wrote my Crested

MY LIFE WITH CRANES

Ibis paper in 1969, there were only about 20 known survivors in Japan, all living on Sado Island. At that time, there had not been reports of ibis on mainland Asia for several decades.

After the ibis landed, I was able to photograph them at a distance and in very poor light. But it confirmed that at least four Crested Ibis survived on the mainland of Asia. The discovery made the news in South Korea, and apparently, North Koreans had some access to South Korean mass media. Birdwatchers (although one is never certain in the DMZ) soon appeared on the fields north of the Military Demarcation Line.

The following winter when I returned to the Panmunjom Valley, there were only two ibis. But to my delight, they spent more time in my study area than during the previous winter. I hoped to finally secure excellent photographs of the rare birds. I made a hiding place from a pile of straw near one of the springs they had visited. One bleak day, freezing winds swept over the DMZ, and the two ibis landed at the spring near my blind. Shivering and with my limited energy pouring into the cold camera and lens, at last I secured good photos of the ibis.

I was in the midst of taking a long series of pictures when they suddenly disappeared from the frame. Still hiding in the straw and looking through the camera, I slowly raised the lens. The frame was now filled by an American soldier with his gun pointed straight at me. Out on patrol, he had flushed the ibis. They had frightened him and it appeared that he was observing the long black object protruding from the straw. Quickly I tightened the lens to its base on the tripod, and I sank down into the rice straw hoping to be a bit protected from an expected hail of bullets. But nothing happened. Apparently, he had not noticed the lens.

Fearing that the ibis might soon disappear for all time, I proposed to the South Korean Government and to the United Nations Command that I be granted permission to capture the last two survivors and to bring them to the Jersey Zoo in England where expertise had been developed in breeding other species of ibis. Permission was granted but before returning to Korea during the winter of 1977, I was invited to speak in Washington at a meeting of the Board of Directors of the World Wildlife Fund.

Always the eternal optimist, I explained that although only two ibis probably remained on the DMZ, perhaps more would someday be located in North Korea and in China and breeding them in captivity might help bolster numbers in the wild. The famed expert on Mountain Gorillas, Diane Fossey, followed my presentation with a depressing account of the tragic death of her favorite Silverback. She publicly disparaged my optimism. Nevertheless, within a few weeks I was back in the DMZ in a hide beside a spring. Mist nets were suspended around the spring in which six decoy ibis stood silently. It was the beginning of one of the longest, coldest, and most boring vigils of my life. For three months from about 8:00 a.m. through 4:00 p.m. when I was allowed in the DMZ, I sat in that hide and waited for the ibis. The nets had to be closed every day before I left and opened when I arrived. And to my chagrin, when cranes appeared I had to appear from the blind and deter them from landing. One crane caught in a mist net would spell the demise of the net. A book of short stories by Mark Twain helped pass those cold and tedious hours.

Finally, I saw the ibis. But there was only one. He appeared in the sky and landed behind a nearby hill. Reasoning that if I flushed the ibis from the area where I thought it landed, it might fly into the neighboring valley, see the decoys, and fly into a net. I left the nets open and walked toward where I hoped I might find the ibis. Sure enough, there he was probing in the mud near a spring where ice had not encroached. Carefully, and from a great distance, I circled the ibis until I stood between it and its easiest flyway back to North Korea. As I slowly approached, he became mildly alert and finally flushed and to my delight, flew over the hill and toward my trap.

Fearing that if captured, the ibis might die from stress and cold if suspended in the mist net, I ran back over the hill to my trapping station. The six decoys had not moved and the nets were empty. A fine mist in the frigid still air had deposited fine ice crystals on the mists nets rendering them stiff and brittle. To my dismay, an opening about the size of an ibis was apparent in one net. My efforts continued, but the ibis never returned and my trapping efforts failed. The next winter, not a single ibis was spotted on the Korean DMZ.

Although my efforts with the Crested Ibis in the DMZ were unsuccessful, these activities helped stimulate conservation action in Japan and in China for the Crested Ibis. In 1981, the five Japanese Crested Ibis survivors were captured using a rocket net (explosives were not allowed in the DMZ, otherwise I might have been successful). That same year, seven wild birds were also discovered in central China. Since then, this population has increased to almost 1,000 in response to conservation efforts and captive breeding and releases. The Crested Ibis is also now breeding again in the wild in Japan.

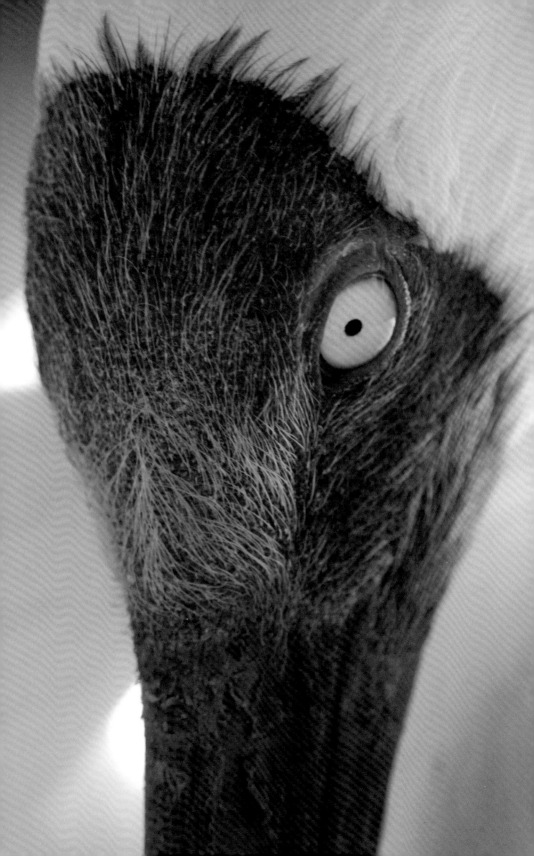

Siberian Cranes

THE LILY OF BIRDS

India was once home to five crane species. Like a huge funnel
beneath Asia, the subcontinent concentrates tens of thousands of migratory
Eurasian and Demoiselle Cranes that breed across Asia including both the
steppes (for the Demoiselles) and the taiga (for the Eurasians). A small group
of Siberian Cranes once migrated from the arctic of western Siberia to India's
Gangetic Plain to spend the winter where the world's tallest flying bird, the
Sarus Crane, is a year-round resident. Unfortunately, the Siberian Crane is
no longer seen in the skies of India. The fifth species is the Black-necked
Crane of the Tibetan Plateau, a small western portion of which lies in a
region of India called Ladakh and provides breeding habitat for a small
population of cranes.

Siberian Cranes and Black-necked Cranes were the only species missing
from my doctoral studies that compared the unison calls of cranes as a
means to shed light on evolutionary relationships. The New York Zoological
Society agreed to sponsor my research of both species in India. However, a
war between India and Pakistan in 1971 was concerning and I decided to
study cranes in Japan instead. I shared my interest in Siberian Cranes with
Ron Sauey. He quickly abandoned his plans to study pheasants. Siberian
Cranes became his passion.

In the early 1970s, it was confirmed that some Siberian Cranes summered in
eastern Siberia and wintered in India. At the time, Russia and the U.S. were
locked in the Cold War, so Ron decided to study the ecology and behavior of

Siberian Cranes at the famous Keoladeo Bird Sanctuary near Bharatpur, India. The fertile Gangetic Plain stretches across northern India between the foothills of the Himalayas and southern drier areas.

During the heyday of the British Raj, the multi-talented administrator and naturalist Alexander Octavian Hume found Siberian Cranes on wetlands near the town of Etawah southeast of Delhi. Noting their exquisite beauty, mate fidelity, and the care lavished on their young, Hume dubbed them the "Lily of Birds." Ron fondly referred to them as the "Sibes." Devotion to their partners is legendary, as depicted in the epic poem *The Ramayana*.

The Maharajah of Bharatpur created the wetlands in the 19th century by diverting monsoon water from a nearby river. Royal hunts sometimes claimed several thousand birds in one day. When India gained its independence in 1949, much of the land in the Kingdom of Bharatpur was taken from the Maharajah and given to the local people. India's foremost ornithologist and conservationist Dr. Salim Ali understood the importance of the area. He persuaded Prime Minister Nehru to protect the area as a sanctuary administered by the State of Rajasthan. In the early days of the new sanctuary, Dr. Ali was aware that Sibes wintered at Bharatpur but he was unaware of their critically endangered status.

RON AND THE SIBES

During the winter of 1973-74, Ron began his comprehensive work on 75 Sibes at Keoladeo. After he started his research, a great interest in the "Lily of Birds" blossomed. Each autumn after their arrival was announced by the media, thousands of visitors flocked to Bharatpur to see the Sibes. In 1974, one of these people was none other than Prime Minister Indira Gandhi, a wildlife enthusiast.

In the mid-1960s, about 200 Siberian Cranes were counted at Bharatpur. When Ron began his research there a decade later, there were only 75, and their numbers continued to decline each year. In early March of 2002, the last pair circled high in the clear spring skies to begin their long migration.

In June, they were sighted on the wetland they had frequented for many years in arctic Russia, but they were never seen again. The extirpation of this Central Asian population of Siberian Cranes was a great loss to the world and especially to India.

During two winters in the mid-1970s, Ron lived in a small cabin at the headquarters of the sanctuary. Most mornings before sunup, he peddled his creaky bicycle along the central dike into the heart of the sanctuary. Chaining the bike to a tree, Ron took off his trousers and stepped into the mud and cold water. His tiny canvas blind was atop a table in the middle of the favorite wetland feeding area of the Sibes. Throughout the day, he meticulously recorded observations that became the basis for his doctoral thesis. Ron was thrilled to be so close to the cranes.

At night, all the Sibes stood together silently in the shallows of a wetland most distant from dikes and roads and thus as distant as possible from terrestrial predators. At dawn, in small groups they dispersed to feeding areas in many different wetlands. Often if a pair had a juvenile, they defended daytime feeding areas against the intrusion of other Sibes. Occasionally, they even battled with their larger relative, the Sarus Crane, and won!

Sibes have the longest beaks of all cranes. At the end of each mandible are tiny serrations that help the bird probe in the mud and grasp the nutritious roots and tubers of aquatic plants. Ron discovered that juveniles remained with their parents throughout the winter, standing nearby as the adults dug in the mud. Although a chick sometimes probed for food, it often waited for the success of its parents. When an adult secured a food item, with head lowered the chick emitted a piercing call that sounding like a loud "weep" which translates, "Give me that food." As winter progressed, the chicks begged less.

During his months of observations in India, Ron noticed that the abundant Sarus and Eurasian Cranes fed on gleanings in the agricultural fields outside the sanctuary, while the Sibes always foraged in the wetlands. Ron concluded that this dependence on wetlands was perhaps a major limiting factor for Siberian Cranes in India and elsewhere. Ron's astute observations advanced the understanding of this critically endangered crane. Although there was ample habitat in the wetlands at Keoladeo Bird Sanctuary, and on the wetlands near Etawah where Hume had observed them a century before, the Sibes continued to decrease. Something was happening elsewhere that was reducing their numbers.

Ron studied 56 cranes during the winter of 1976-77, 20 fewer than when he first met the Indian flock two years earlier. Among the 56 birds were eight pairs with a chick in tow. When they arrived, the chicks were predominantly cinnamon brown, but over the winter, at varying rates, they shed their juvenile plumage and turned white. By mid-March, few brown feathers remained. However, there was enough incomplete and uneven molting that Ron could easily identify each of the chicks as individuals and thus each of the crane families.

After the cranes migrated north in March, Ron went to Lake Ab-e-Estada in Afghanistan to search for them. He found a flock of 55 cranes that included the eight families he had observed throughout the winter. Ron felt like he was reunited with old friends. He also reported that Eurasian Cranes were

being sold for their meat in the markets. He concluded that hunting along the migration route was likely the primary reason for the decline of the group that migrated to India.

Ron captured the complex body language of the Sibes on film, and he recorded their vigorous calls. He studied the relationships between the cranes and the villagers who grazed herds of cattle and buffalo in the sanctuary. In 1985, he presented comprehensive historical information about Siberian Cranes, and new details of their behavior and ecology in his doctoral dissertation. How fortunate this body of information was collected before the demise of the population.

Ron's life in India was enriched through close friendships with filmmakers Belinda (Blue) Wright and Stanley Breeden. They met at Bharatpur in 1977 when the Breedens were shooting a documentary film, *Birds of the Indian Monsoon.* Through this film, the charm of the sanctuary, including spectacular footage of Siberian Cranes, has been shared with millions.

On Christmas Day in 1986, while preparing dinner for his family, Ron, age 38, suffered a cerebral hemorrhage and passed away several weeks later. As a close friend wrote at the time, "He was the best of us." It was true. He had always been the perfect host for the many students, volunteers, and visitors that came from far and wide. Ron's monumental doctoral research on Siberian Cranes still stands as the most outstanding document ever compiled on this most endangered crane species. Ron and his parents played a vital role in creating the International Crane Foundation. In Ron's memory, his family supported the construction of the Ron Sauey Memorial Library for Bird Conservation at ICF. Surrounded by his books, artwork and photographs – his spirit is present there.

ZHENG ZHONGJIE

RECOVERING UNDER
AN ACACIA TREE

The winter between Ron's Indian visits to Bharatpur, I was in Iran capturing and color-marking about 90 Eurasian Cranes. At the end of that challenging field assignment, while living in a remote village where hepatitis was common, I contracted the disease. Several children had succumbed, and I was concerned for my own life. At that time, my normal weight was 165

MY LIFE WITH CRANES

pounds. At a doctor's office in Shiraz, I weighed in at 103 pounds and it was difficult to hold up my head. Liquids, fruit, and several months of rest at home were the strong recommendations of a doctor in Tehran.

The Director of the Iran Department of the Environment was delighted by our success with the Eurasian Cranes. As a bonus, he offered two Iranian colleagues and me an expedition to India to study the Sibes. I felt in my spirit that being with the wild Sibes and bathed in the warm winter sunshine of India might bring rapid healing to my distended liver. Two days later, I was in India reclining under an acacia tree at Bharatpur. Bholu Khan, a keen naturalist, photographer, and charming gentleman employed at the reserve, was most helpful as he had been to Ron the previous winter. In addition to directing me to prime spots to observe the cranes, Bholu often visited by bicycle to provide delicious fresh fruits, custards, sandwiches and sweetened white tea in a thermos. Bholu and the cranes helped heal me, and within a few days, I forgot I was ill.

HUMMOCK NUMBER 15

Eventually, we built a blind on a hummock (a mound rising above the wetland) near the roost of the cranes. Arriving before dawn, I had a unique opportunity to be near the Sibes and the other wildlife of one of earth's greatest reserves. Several times a pair of magnificent Black-necked Storks landed nearby and performed their wing-shaking, bill-clattering courtship display. I was alarmed when a Sambar Deer with a splendid rack walked into the frame of my 600 mm lens. My strength returned with a surge.

The hummock that supported my blind was one of dozens of hummocks that dotted portions of the wetlands. Acacia trees planted on the hummocks provided excellent nesting habitat for colonial aquatic birds that included cormorants, darters, ibis, spoonbills, herons, egrets, and storks. These birds mostly nested during the summer monsoons. In the winter, the water levels in the sanctuary were dropping and with the exception of great numbers of Painted Storks, most of the nests were empty.

There was a mystery I wanted to solve.

In the evening, only a portion of the Siberian Cranes returned to the roosting area beside the acacia mounds. However, in the morning, all the cranes were at the roost beside the mounds. In other species of cranes, the birds fly to the safety of the roost before dusk. When did the remainder of these Siberian Cranes fly back to the roost? In an effort to answer that question, I spent a night in the blind.

As predicted, some of the cranes returned in late afternoon probed a bit, loafed, preened, and then as darkness came, rested their heads on their backs with their bills tucked under a wing. All was silent. Not long after the stars appeared, I heard many Siberian Cranes flying low overhead. It was too dark to see if cranes were still at the roost. It sounded like many were in the air. The flock circled widely several times and then they all plunked down in the shallows near my blind. Mystery solved. Unfortunately, the fog was thick in the morning and photography was impossible.

Very early the following morning, an hour before first light, I left my cabin and with camera and tripod loaded in my backpack, I took a bicycle into the sleeping sanctuary. At a predetermined spot, in the dark, I slowly took off my shoes and pants and cautiously and silently waded barefoot into the cold shallows. Afraid that I might frighten the cranes, I moved slowly and quietly, aware that one step might take me into the deeper water of the pits that surrounded each hummock. My cold feet sank deep in the mud and plants brushed against my legs in the knee-deep water. The tops of the acacia trees were faintly visible against the stars. I knew that the hummock with my blind was the fifteenth from my departure point. My limitations in foreign languages are second only to my limitations in mathematics. Believing mound number 14 to be mound number 15, I approached at a snail's pace, fearing that the cranes might hear me and flush. Step by silent step I approached that mound – extending my hand to touch the canvas of the blind. But, instead of touching canvas, I touched the warm back of a sleeping Nilgai, a large member of the antelope family. Responding as if it was escaping from a tiger, it bellowed loudly, HONK! It exploded from the hummock into the shallows. I nearly fainted with fright. The water was up to my waist now. My knees started shaking and I feared I might collapse into the water with my cameras. Then came the sickening thought that surely the Sibes had heard the commotion and departed.

After recovering a bit, I cautiously approached the next hummock, the real number 15. I crawled from the water apprehensive that an enormous python might be lurking inside the blind. To check, I extended the folded legs of my

tripod through the door and probed around to confirm the absence of unwanted company. Soon I was prepared for photography.

Apparently, the cranes were accustomed to the honks of Nilgai. As the first light of dawn arrived, I could see large white motionless objects in the water about 100 yards away. The cranes had not flown. Three started to move to the right. Perhaps a family group was leaving. Wanting to photograph the entire flock at their roost, with 600 mm lens firmly mounted on the tripod, I moved the lens from right to left and I took eight exposures of what I believed to be the cranes. It was too dark to see the birds clearly, so each frame was exposed for a half second. The sensitive film detected the flock much better than the naked eye. By chance, the exposure was excellent. When I returned to ICF, Ron and I pieced the eight pictures together. There were 55 cranes and they now stand framed in the Ron Sauey Library at the International Crane Foundation.

MEETING INDIRA GANDHI

It was the opinion of Ron Sauey and Dr. Salim Ali that the bird sanctuary at Bharatpur was deteriorating. Twelve extremely poor villages surrounded the 7,000-acre sanctuary. Every morning hundreds of villagers led thousands of cattle and buffalo into the sanctuary to graze. Every evening the herds were driven home by attendants carrying large loads of firewood. Although hunting was strictly forbidden in the sanctuary, Ron often witnessed poachers shooting geese and ducks. It appeared that the sanctuary was being overrun, a concern I expressed during a memorable audience with Prime Minister Indira Gandhi during the summer of 1982.

That July the heat was intense. The Bharatpur sanctuary had dried up, and the colonial water birds were elsewhere awaiting the return of the monsoon. The Sibes were among millions of mosquitoes on their breeding grounds in the arctic. I was in Delhi developing plans for an international workshop on cranes that we hoped to convene in Bharatpur in February of 1983. My confidant and helper, Belinda Wright, suggested we discuss the problems at Bharatpur with the Prime Minister. Since childhood, Mrs. Gandhi had an interest in wildlife and was once the leader of the Bird Watching Club in Delhi. After she assumed leadership of the world's largest democracy, she chaired the Indian Board for Wildlife and in 1972, the Wildlife Conservation Act was passed. Through her leadership, the Government of India and the World Wildlife Fund joined forces to save the tigers. Perhaps she could intervene on behalf of the cranes.

Mrs. Gandhi's secretary informed us that five days hence Belinda and I were scheduled to have a meeting in the evening with the Prime Minister at her residence. We meticulously developed a colorful album describing the

Bharatpur Sanctuary, the Sibes, and the problems. Hours before the meeting, it was rescheduled for the following evening, a pattern repeated three times before we finally met the Prime Minister. I was apprehensive about meeting Mrs. Gandhi. It was 1982, and the U.S. was actively supporting India's rival, Pakistan, since the Soviets invaded Afghanistan in 1979. Relations between India and the U.S. were strained. I reasoned that the last thing the Prime Minister likely wanted was a person from the U.S. telling her about a problem in India.

Mrs. Gandhi and entourage were attending a reception for the navy when Belinda and I passed through security at the front gate of the compound in which her residence was located. Armed with a slide projector and the album, we were ushered into a huge parlor with several large cushioned easy chairs and a sofa around a fireplace. Toward the back of the room were several rows of straight-backed chairs. Reasoning that Mrs. Gandhi would sit at the front in one of the easy chairs, we set up the screen in front of the fireplace and displayed our album on a coffee table.

Maneka Gandhi, Mrs. Gandhi's daughter-in-law, was the first to arrive. Her husband and heir-apparent, Sanjay, had recently perished in a plane crash. She and their child lived with the Prime Minister. I was amazed by Maneka's interest in conservation. A decade later, she became the Minister of the Environment. Eventually the Prime Minister, encased in a light blue veil-like sari arrived in the company of a white-robed guru, her eldest son Rajiv, his wife Sonia, their children, and several aids. Totally inexperienced in greeting a Prime Minister, I walked up to Mrs. Gandhi, extended my hand and blurted out, "Hello, Mrs. Gandhi. I'm George Archibald from the International Crane Foundation in Baraboo, Wisconsin." She politely shook my hand but remained silent.

Next, I invited her to sit down in the easy chair and look at my slides. But she preferred to view slides from afar and proceeded to go to the back of the room and sit down in one of the straight-backed chairs. I followed. The presentation went without a hitch. There were pictures of the rivers, forests and wetlands where Russian scientist Dr. Alexander Sorokin discovered the breeding grounds of the Sibes the previous summer. When I shared a photo of a dead crane hanging in a market in Afghanistan and mentioned that little could be done to protect the cranes against hunting when war was raging, Mrs. Gandhi stiffened. I praised conservation programs in India and indicated that the long-term welfare of the Siberian Cranes at the sanctuary near Bharatpur could be strengthened if practices by the local people could be managed in a sustainable manner. I suggested banning the cutting of large trees and hunting, and controlling grazing. I also thought that his might be achieved if the sanctuary was administered nationally rather than as a state reserve.

After the slides, I showed her a map of China and the location of the newly discovered wintering grounds of the eastern flock of Siberian Cranes. After mentioning that she had another appointment, she disappeared into the night. It had been a strained meeting and were it not for uplifting input from Belinda at strategic moments, it would have definitely been much worse. After Mrs. Gandhi left, Rajiv, Maneka, Sonia, and their friends, revived my sinking spirits. We chatted for about an hour and Rajiv invited us to seek his assistance if it was needed in the future. But I was not pleased with the meeting. Mrs. Gandhi had said very little and she seemed remote. Belinda and I went to the restaurant at the Imperial Hotel and ordered stiff drinks. We were exhausted. Had we done more damage than good?

Three weeks later big news broke that Maneka would be heading an opposition party to Mrs. Gandhi's Congress Party and that Mrs. Gandhi had asked Maneka to move from the residence of the Prime Minister. The separate arrivals of Maneka and Mrs. Gandhi on the evening of our meeting, and the tensions we felt, were perhaps in part a consequence of the conflict between them.

CONFLICT AT THE SANCTUARY

For many years, the Government of India had been aware of the problems at Bharatpur. Most of India's nature reserves feel the impact of the escalating numbers of humanity. A high wall was erected around the entire sanctuary to prevent use of the sanctuary by villagers, but particularly in times of drought, holes were made in the wall giving the locals access to grazing, firewood, and water.

In the autumn of 1982, after our meeting and before the Siberian Cranes returned, Mrs. Gandhi ordered that the walls around the sanctuary be repaired and that guards be posted at the gates to control the use of the sanctuary. The Government would provide dry fodder for the livestock. In January, the local people gathered at the front gates of the sanctuary to protest the decision. They started throwing rocks at the police and received live fire in return and seven villagers were killed. But the Government remained firm in its stand against overuse of the sanctuary. Eventually the Bharatpur Bird Sanctuary was declared Keoladeo National Park, India's first wetland national park.

Although cattle can overpopulate and denude upland habitats, water buffalo are a natural and important component of the ecology of wetlands on the Gangetic Plains. The buffalo eat aquatic vegetation that otherwise might dominate a region and limit the use of the area by wildlife. Although a herd of feral cattle remained within the wall that surrounded Keoladeo, all buffalo were removed. In retrospect, a small herd should have been left to control the aggressive grasses. But the authorities had an all or nothing approach to the buffalo grazing. Within a few years, many of the wetlands were clogged with plants and scraping off the grasses with bulldozers during the dry season was needed to provide proper habitat for Sibes in winter.

In February 1983, to draw attention to the plight of the Siberian Cranes and promote international cooperation in conservation, ICF and the government of India co-hosted an International Crane Workshop. It was just a few months after the bloodbath at the front gate. Needless to say, I was a bit apprehensive bringing 89 of the world's top crane people into a potentially dangerous situation. But we were blessed with peace, excellent weather, and Sibes foraging near the colorful tent that housed the meeting. For the first time, Russian and Chinese experts had a chance to meet. Four years had passed since the Iranian Revolution and my Iranian colleagues and I had a joyous reunion. The meeting was the genesis of the European Working Group on Cranes and the African Working Group Cranes. Even a stamp was released that featured Siberian Cranes.

A HATCH HEARD
AROUND THE WORLD!

In 1976, there was only one critically endangered Siberian Crane in the U.S. Her name was Phyllis, and she arrived in Baraboo on breeding loan that summer, after more than 30 years at the Philadelphia Zoo. For many years, she had been on display in a rather small enclosure shared with waterfowl. At ICF, she was given a large, grassy, private enclosure, and a house. The space, solitude, and stimulation from other pairs of cranes displaying nearby stimulated Phyllis to begin performing a series of calls we later described as pre-copulatory calls. We sensed her motivation to become reproductively active.

An old male Siberian Crane, thought to have hatched in 1905, survived both world wars living in a zoo in Switzerland. Wolf and Ushi Brehm, the founders and owners of the great bird park Vogelpark Walsrode in Germany, later acquired him. I visited the Brehms in 1976 and saw the old crane now named Wolf. On a frigid and windy night in November of that year, Wolf arrived on breeding loan in Baraboo, Wisconsin. He was 71 years old at the time! As we lifted the plywood crate that contained Wolf and took him from the van, Phyllis began calling. Wolf answered from the crate. It was an incredibly touching moment to hear two birds communicating that had not heard the voice of their own species for many decades.

They were placed in adjacent enclosures and immediately appeared to be attracted to each other. Within a few weeks, Wolf was placed with Phyllis. Their enclosure was lined with old Christmas trees to provide the ambiance of the Russian taiga where some Siberian Cranes nest. As with the Hooded Cranes, floodlights were installed to simulate the almost continual daylight to which Siberian Cranes are exposed on their breeding grounds during late spring and summer. When they started painting the bases of their necks with dirt in what appeared to be a sexual display, we provided a bucket of black marsh mud to mimic a more natural substance. I cherish the memory of watching Phyllis and Wolf late at night with their enclosure bathed in bright light and engaging in bursts of activity including dancing, nest building, and long bouts of pre-copulatory calling that sometimes ended with actual copulation. To our delight, Phyllis laid her first egg! We collected the eggs as

they were laid to encourage continued production. To our amazement, they produced 12 eggs, but unfortunately, all the eggs were infertile.

There was a lone Siberian Crane in captivity at the Hirakawa Zoo in Japan. Blown off course during migration, the juvenile female was rescued by children and rehabilitated at the zoo. She was named Hirakawa and she matured into a magnificent bird. Believed to be a male at the time, Hirakawa was sent to ICF as a semen donor for Phyllis. When placed in a nearby enclosure, Hirakawa began displaying with Wolf, not Phyllis. I immediately subdivided the enclosure containing the pair, with Wolf occupying the pen between the two females.

That spring, Hirakawa began laying eggs, but despite our efforts with artificial insemination, the eggs were infertile. To increase the chances of fertility, a second old male was imported from Germany, and in 1981, we achieved the first captive breeding of Siberian Cranes. We named the chick

"Dushenka," which means "little loved one" in Russian. We were honored to receive a congratulatory letter from Indira Gandhi. It was a hatch heard around the world! Wolf later produced viable semen samples, and is listed in the Siberian Crane studbook as the sire of two chicks in 1982. Five years later at the age of 82, Wolf died. His longevity record is chronicled in the 35th edition of the *Guinness Book of Records*.

प्रधान मंत्री भवन
PRIME MINISTER'S HOUSE
NEW DELHI

June 2, 1982

Dear Mr. Archibald,

I had just scribbled a reply to your letter of the 24th when your next letter dated 25th arrived.

I am delighted to hear of your success in breeding Siberian cranes and the survival of the little ones.

I wish I could come to your Foundation. It would have been a relaxing change from the usual routine of State visits. But my schedule is so rushed that it is not possible to add to it or to go to another town.

Yours sincerely,

(Indira Gandhi)

Mr. George Archibald,
Director,
International Crane Foundation,
City View Road,
Baraboo, Wisconsin 53913
U.S.A.

THE CZAR OF RUSSIAN CRANES

In the beginning, our work in Russia was built on a close personal friendship Ron and I developed with one of the world's leading ornithologists, Professor Vladimir Flint. How a unique and powerful chemistry developed between this distinguished and warm-hearted aristocrat in a classless society and two obscure graduate students from an era of hippies in a free society, remains a delightful mystery. Perhaps such warmth emerged as a response to the contrast between our nations during the Cold War. We seemed to instinctively know it was vital that we join together to help the most endangered of cranes, the Siberian Crane.

Russia is an important home for seven species of cranes. Tens of thousands of Eurasian and Demoiselle Cranes populate the taiga and grasslands, while perhaps 40,000 Sandhill Cranes breed in northeast Siberia. Threatened Hooded, White-naped, and Red-crowned Cranes inhabit southeast Siberia while the elusive and rare Siberian Crane breeds exclusively in northern areas of Russia. All of Russia's cranes are migratory and through these migrations, the cranes link Russia with many nations in Africa, Eurasia, and North America.

Unlike the cosmopolitan cranes, the Russians have a history of insularity. During the era of the czars, without special permission, diplomats were not allowed to travel from the confines of their embassies. Likewise, Russians seldom ventured outside national borders. Within this context, how could American and Russian conservationists work together? In 1972, to help relieve tensions between the superpowers, Russia and the U.S. signed an Environment Agreement whereby specialists from the two nations could work together on approved programs. Perhaps this agreement could help the cranes? With a twinkle in his eye, Flint always called it our "engine."

After a series of letters with Flint about cranes in general and Siberian Cranes in particular, I arrived in Moscow, fresh from the field in Iran, on a cold snowy evening in March of 1976. I was met by a very nervous Russian-speaking U.S. volunteer, Libby Anderson. In a subdued voice she recommended that, to make our meeting at the airport seem more natural, we pretend to be a couple. The next morning we met Dr. Flint at his dark little office in a back room in the Zoological Museum. Middle-aged, barrel-chested, bearded, soft-spoken, and refined, he seemed quite shy. With Libby as interpreter, we shared stories about his work on Siberian Cranes on their breeding grounds in Yakutia and my recent studies in Iran of Eurasian Cranes.

Dr. Flint's partnership was vital for our proposal to Soviet and American officials that hatching eggs from wild Siberian Cranes be exported to the U.S. to start a captive colony at ICF. I believed we could induce captive Siberian Cranes to lay their eggs in synchrony with wild Eurasian Cranes by exposing the Siberian Cranes in late winter and early spring to artificial lighting to simulate arctic photoperiod conditions. It was also important to establish a viable captive population of Siberian Cranes. At that time, the tiny remnant flock that wintered in Iran had not yet been discovered. The flock that wintered in India was in steep decline and the wintering grounds of the birds that wintered in China was still a mystery. It was a long and complicated

argument filled with conditionals, but Flint liked it and was soon on the telephone with Dr. Vasily Vasilovitch Krinitski, the official in the Ministry of Agriculture responsible for Russian–American projects under the Environmental Agreement.

To prove that crane eggs could be safely transported long distances, in 1974, my colleagues in Sweden sent to ICF six Eurasian Crane eggs in the final stages of incubation. The eggs were transported on commercial flights in a small plywood box with an inner lining of Styrofoam. Two horizontal pieces of thick foam each with matching egg sized depressions, were sandwiched between layers of foam rubber. A narrow hinged door on the outside of the box opened into a chamber where hot water bottles could be placed beneath the foam rubber and Styrofoam. A thermometer extended into the egg chambers. All six eggs from Sweden hatched and we reared all six chicks. It was a resounding success and through correspondence, I had shared all the details with Dr. Flint.

To promote the idea of the egg lift over the Iron Curtain, some weeks before my arrival in Moscow, ICF sent Dr. Flint the same egg box that was used in Sweden. A professional bureaucrat, Dr. Krinitski was a short, rotund, bald, and vivacious man who shared a friendship with Dr. Flint. Not long after the phone conversation with Flint, Dr. Krinitski joined us wearing a snow-covered fur hat and a long black coat. He seemed like the perfect Russian stereotype. After greetings, Dr. Flint pulled a bottle of vodka from his desk and we shared a toast before embarking upon an explanation of the egg box and the complex long-term project for which the box was an ambassador. The Russian word for the Siberian Crane is "sterkh." That week in Moscow in

1976 marked the official beginning of Project Sterkh. Although it was illegal for a foreigner to visit a Russian home back then, that evening we were served an excellent meal of roast saiga antelope at the residence of the Flints.

In June of 1977, Dr. Flint and his colleague, Dr. Alexander Sorokin, took the egg box to the tundra of Yakutia in eastern Siberia to search for Siberian Crane nests from a helicopter. Thick fog settled over the wetlands and it was impossible to conduct the surveys. By the time the weather improved, most of the eggs in the wild nests had hatched. Luckily, they eventually located two nests with eggs and all four eggs were carefully placed in the egg box. Libby Anderson met Flint in Moscow and cared for the eggs on the flight to the United States. Forty-eight hours after they were collected and following a 10,000-mile journey, the eggs were placed in a heated chamber in a quarantine facility at the University of Wisconsin. Viability of a late embryo can be tested by floating the egg in lukewarm water. If the embryo is alive, it moves and its egg moves too. If it is not a viable embryo, the egg floats motionless. Two eggs from one nest were both motionless. A subsequent examination indicated they were perhaps infertile or that the embryo had died in the early stages of development. There was no fault attributed to transport. The second clutch of eggs was alive! Both hatched in mid-July and the two chicks, both female, were reared. We named them Vladimira and Kyta, the former after Flint and the latter after the area in Siberia where Siberian Cranes nest.

COLD WAR
WARM FRIENDSHIP

In May 1978, our foremost Russian colleague Dr. Vladimir Flint visited the International Crane Foundation for the first time. He was anxious to see the two Siberian Cranes we had reared from eggs carried 10,000 miles from the breeding grounds in Siberia. We hoped to import more eggs that year, but questioned the wisdom of such action considering the disease situation at ICF in 1978. Believing that the disease was under control and that measures could be taken to prevent its spread, we decided to proceed with the import of additional Siberian Crane eggs. The fragile state of relations between the U.S. and the USSR further confirmed that we should proceed with the import, while it remained a possibility under the aegis of the Environment Agreement.

In early July, Ron arrived in Madison gently carrying a suitcase containing hot water bottles, four incubating Siberian Crane eggs, and one newly hatched chick named Aeroflot. The chick had been peeping in the shell in Moscow and hatched over Cleveland, Ohio. I reared the chicks at a specially prepared quarantine facility provided in the Biotron at the University of Wisconsin.

Dr. Flint's understudy, Dr. Alexander (Sasha) Sorokin studied Siberian Cranes with Flint at the All-Soviet Institute for Nature Conservation. Sasha Sorokin was a young man in 1978 when in a van parked near Red Square, he showed me the locations of nests of Siberian Cranes on a military map that was completely forbidden for foreign eyes. He had just returned from aerial surveys of the tundra in Yakutia in eastern Siberia. It was the beginning of a long friendship that continues to this day. A year later, the Soviets invaded Afghanistan driving the temperature of the Cold War to an all-time low. The U.S. discontinued most cooperative programs with the USSR except for the Environmental Agreement, reasoning that a tiny web of connection should be maintained in case relations improved. In a quiet moment during a visit to Russia that year, I asked Flint what he thought about the Afghanistan situation. Taking a deep drag on his ubiquitous cigarette, he exhaled with the words, "They didn't ask me."

Flint and his colleagues at Oka Nature Reserve wanted to establish a captive breeding center for the four crane species of the Soviet Union. Oka was one of the many strictly protected nature reserves scattered across the vast USSR. Visitation except for staff and special guests was forbidden. Nature thrived without disturbance from humans. As a first step in establishing a breeding center, ICF had sent a small but excellent electric incubator to the Russians to be used to hatch Siberian Crane eggs collected from wild birds and transported to the newly established center at Oka. Five Siberian Cranes hatched and they named the oldest one George and later Georgina when they determined George was a female! Flint remarked that the best way to determine a crane chick's sex was to give it a name, and it would end up being the opposite sex.

About 200 miles south of Moscow, the Pra River is a tiny western tributary of the mighty Oka River. The winding Pra provides swamps where many pairs of Eurasian Cranes nest and once provided remote solitude for a notorious pirate named Brykin. Living in a cabin near the Pra in the heart of the wilderness, Brykin ventured out to the Oka River to plunder. Oka Nature Reserve was established many years after the demise of this pirate, but the homes of the scientists, administrators, and guards for the reserve were constructed near the site of Brykin's cabin. It became Brykin Bor ("Bor" is the Russian word for village). Since my first visit in 1978, it has been like a home to me and later to others from ICF.

Dr. Svet Preklonski, a waterfowl biologist and the Director of Oka at that time, always provided a warm welcome. The leader of the captive breeding center was a Ukrainian ornithologist Vladimir Panchenko. Vladimir had a small black Cocker Spaniel named Friend. To me, Friend came to symbolize the trust and the warmth of the friendships I developed with my Russian colleagues, especially with Flint and Panchenko. High points of each visit were meals at the homes of Preklonski and Panchenko. It seemed that the farther from Moscow I traveled, the more acceptable such events became.

At least one and sometimes two KGB officials accompanied Flint and me on our annual trips to Oka. Although they were pleasant enough people, I always had a funny feeling about them. It was like having a plainclothes police officer trying to participate in activities about which he knew or cared very little. I once caused great stress in the mind of our "associate" when I left an observation crane blind to relieve myself. We had been waiting for hours and the wild cranes did not appear. I did not return immediately, but lingered for some time near the blind observing songbirds – perhaps a little too long. The associate was upset – he thought I was spying.

MY LIFE WITH CRANES

We wanted to study rare cranes in the field too, but it was almost impossible for foreigners to travel to the remote areas in the arctic and near the border with China where the Siberian, Red-crowned, White-naped, and Hooded Cranes nested. Consequently, it was always a joy in Moscow to meet with field researchers in autumn or winter after they returned from their adventures with the wild cranes during spring and summer. Sasha and Flint were always interested to hear my news about the Siberian Cranes in India. The Indian population was declining. Ron Sauey had found them during migration at a lake in central Afghanistan, and there were scattered reports of the species during migration in Uzbekistan and Kazakhstan. Farther north, they disappeared. Their breeding ground remained a mystery until Sasha discovered it in 1981.

Flint's work with Siberian Cranes and the captive breeding center at Oka Nature Reserve was well known throughout Russia. That year news was sent to Flint that a woman in a village along the Ob River in western Siberia had a pet Siberian Crane. Sasha traveled by helicopter to the remote village of Gorki and observed a dirty juvenile Siberian Crane living with a pack of dogs at the home of a woman named Tatiana. As a small chick, the lone crane had walked up to a group of boaters who were picnicking on a sandbar in the Ob River. The boaters knew that Tatiana loved animals. Now, she had a crane to raise. The crane and the dogs became friends and spent nights together in a crawl space under the house. On a diet of fish, the crane's feathers became oiled and dirty. It was an otherwise healthy Siberian Crane that Sasha tucked under his jacket and carried to the waiting helicopter as snow began to fly. Hours later, "Sauey" was in Flint's bathtub in Moscow. He later joined the other captive cranes at Oka. The following spring, Sasha, a pilot, and friend Sasha Ermakov returned for an aerial survey of the region where Sauey had been found as a flightless juvenile. To their delight they found several nesting pairs of Siberian Cranes, a population that through later color-banding proved to be the same treasured cranes that wintered in India.

The friendship between Vladimir Flint, Ron, and me was the fundamental ingredient that helped assure the success of our work during the Cold War. Libby Anderson wrote her thesis at Cornell University on the machinations of collaboration within the terms of the Environment Agreement between our nations. I asked Flint for his opinion about Libby's eloquent analysis. He had an interesting and profound comment, "Dear Libby missed the most important point. Although the bilateral work was historic and important, the reason it worked was because of our close friendship!"

KUNOVAT BASIN,
WESTERN SIBERIA

In 1990, I spent, along with my Russian friends, a month living in tents on a forested island surrounded by lakes and wetlands and within one kilometer of the nest of one of the last two breeding pairs of Siberian Cranes in this population. To share such a remarkable experience with close friends in formerly forbidden lands amidst cranes and a plethora of other wildlife was an experience of a lifetime. The weather cycles were dramatic with wind and rain for several days followed by clear skies, little wind, and millions of mosquitoes. We rested in our tents during the bad weather. When conditions improved, we worked almost 24 hours a day in that glorious land of the midnight sun.

Flint searched for the nests of waxwings, Sasha observed the cranes at the nest, while others captured and placed a satellite radio transmitter on a wild Eurasian Crane. I spent quality time in several hides observing cranes, loons, ducks, geese, raptors, shorebirds, and songbirds. I will always cherish the memory of the male Siberian Crane suddenly appearing low over my hide in a descending flight to the nest. He glided down on motionless wings that cut through the air with a loud whistling sound.

Over the next decade, many captive-reared birds were released near the last of the wild Siberian and Eurasian Cranes on the basin of the Kunovat River. They usually joined the wild cranes and migrated. However, they did not appear on the wintering grounds in India and were not confirmed on the breeding grounds in subsequent years. The last pair of Siberian Cranes was seen on these wetlands in the summer of 2002.

THE CASPIAN LOWLANDS
OF IRAN

In February of 1978, the wintering area of the Siberian Cranes
that breed in Russia was discovered in waterfowl trapping areas called
damgahs on the Caspian lowlands of Iran. Word reached me in South Korea
where I had spent the winter trying to capture a single Crested Ibis on the
DMZ. On my way home in late February, I had a three-day stop in Iran to
see the newly discovered Siberian Cranes.

On the Caspian lowlands, ducks and geese rest in safe areas throughout the
day and at night fly out to other fields and wetlands to feed. Centuries ago,
the local people developed ingenious methods for trapping them. The
damgah consists of a central flooded and secure area where the birds rest
during the day, bordered by a wall of reed mats and a narrow track of forest.
Within each trapping unit, there is a small cabin, a shelter, and pond for a
decoy flock of domestic but strong-flying mallard ducks, and various traps.
Disturbance of the birds in the damgah is strictly prohibited and visitors are
not welcomed.

Unfortunately, I arrived on a weekend and my colleagues were unable to join me in the journey from Tehran over the Alborz Mountains to the lowlands. So, with scripted cards in English and Persian with critical questions, I traveled all day alone by bus to the coastal town of Feredun Keenar. The cranes were rumored to live in the heart of a nearby damgah.

Fortunately, a kind and English-speaking taxi driver named Ali stopped and offered to help me. During the next 24 hours, he provided conversation, transportation, accommodations, and translation during an interview with the police. Iran was about to burst into revolution and security was intense. I showed the police my cards and asked for their assistance. They chuckled, politely nodded, and released me. It was pouring rain the next morning and our inspection of a small damgah near the home of Ali's friend did not reveal cranes although the trappers claimed that a few cranes sometimes appeared.

It was his day off so Ali remained with his friends. He gave the taxi keys to his cousin Safa and asked that Safa drive me to other areas. For hours, in blinding rain and bad roads we unsuccessfully searched for damgahs. Late in the afternoon, the sky cleared. As we returned to Safa's hometown of Feredun Keenar, I observed a man walking from the fields along a narrow and muddy path carrying a load of dead ducks. I left Safa and followed the path. In the distance were trees. Maneuvering to a vantage point where I could see the wide-open area between the two major rows of trees, I was thrilled to spot about 50 large white dots in the distance. Adrenaline surged. Could they be Siberian Cranes? Closer examination by telescope revealed pelicans.

I continued to trudge along through rice fields that bordered one line of trees. As I approached the trees hoping for a glimpse into the central area, two trappers appeared from the undergrowth, gesticulated, and waved that I depart. I responded by waving my cards. With brows deeply furrowed, they silently approached. Proudly, I displayed my cards. But they seemed to be illiterate. It was dusk and soon would be dark. This was my only day in the field. I was so near yet so very far away. Then the familiar unison call of a pair of Siberian Cranes lifted from the other side of the trees. I had found them! The next morning Ali, Safa, and the police returned with me to negotiate with the trappers. We observed one pair of Siberian Cranes before Ali drove me to the outskirts of Feredun Keenar. Then I hitchhiked back to Tehran to share with my colleagues an account of the exciting adventure.

Ted Thousand

PROFESSOR CHENG

China is home to the world's greatest diversity of cranes – eight of the 15 species. Of these, six are threatened. China's foremost ornithologist was the late Professor Cheng Tso-hsin. Graduating with a Ph.D. from the University of Michigan in 1922, he was the youngest candidate ever to receive such a doctorate from that institution. He married a concert pianist Lydia, and they had four children. Until his death in 1998, Professor Cheng worked tirelessly at the Institute of Zoology in Beijing as the nation's foremost authority on birds.

His major life work was the massive book, *The Birds of China*. Decades in the making, this monumental volume was confiscated and presumed destroyed by Red Guards during the early years of terror of the Cultural Revolution that swept China between 1966 and 1976. However, unlike many of his colleagues who perished, Professor Cheng and his family survived. For several years, he cleaned latrines. As the political sky cleared toward the end of the 1970s, survivors returned to their institutions and miraculously, the rough draft of *The Birds of China* was located in a warehouse.

While I was a graduate student from 1968 -71, I wrote Professor Cheng asking about the status of cranes in China. I received a one line typed reply, "China has eight species of cranes and little is known about their status." After ICF was established in 1973, I wrote to Professor Cheng again and received a similar reply. But his answer came during a period when scholars were persecuted in China. I was relieved that he was alive. In August of 1979, while visiting my family in Nova Scotia, I hand wrote a letter to Professor Cheng explaining that I would be in east Asia in autumn and welcomed an opportunity to visit him if an invitation could be provided. I gave him the address of my hotel in Tokyo and the date that I would be there in early October. My letter carried colorful Canadian stamps.

After working in Russia and South Korea that autumn, I finally arrived at the hotel in Tokyo. There was a letter waiting for me at my hotel. It was from Professor Cheng inviting me to come to Beijing in early November. I soon had a visa and booked a flight to Beijing. It was late in the evening when I arrived at a very dark and dingy airport. An enormous and illuminated portrait of Chairman Mao looked down at the visitor's entrance. Professor Cheng and three colleagues – Ding, Zhou, and Liu – all wearing navy blue Mao suits, greeted me warmly. During the next two years, Ding and Zhou would discover the wintering grounds of Siberian Cranes at Poyang Lake, and Liu would locate seven Crested Ibis breeding near Xian.

The three younger scientists were all smiles but did not speak English. Professor Cheng did all the talking and apologized that his English was "a bit rusty." He was such a warm-hearted and jovial man, I instantly bonded with him. My apprehensions about the visit soon vanished.

A CRACK IN THE WALL

The Friendship Hotel near the Institute of Zoology was to be my home for the next week. That first night I was so excited that I could not sleep. A few Black-necked Cranes, the only species of crane I had never seen, resided at the Beijing Zoo. From a map in the lobby, the zoo appeared to be only several kilometers from the hotel – right for a distance and then left for a distance. The right was easy, but which left? It was pitch dark and street signs if visible were all in Chinese.

Still awake, at about 3:00 a.m., I donned my jogging gear and headed out. At a major intersection, from the left, I heard the distant bugles of cranes – as if they were calling to me. As I jogged along, the infrequent calls became louder until finally I reached a high stone wall that appeared to surround the zoo. By following it, I found the closed and locked entrance gate. Continuing along, I was delighted to discover a large gap in the wall and workmen sleeping on the ground around small fires. Apparently, they were rebuilding that portion of the wall during the day.

Tiptoeing among the sleeping workers, I was soon inside the zoo as the first rays of dawn made it possible to follow paths. Soon I reached a large pond with an island. There were many birds on the water and on the island. With increased light, I could make out the unmistakable form of a Black-necked Crane. What a moment – at long last, to see a Black-necked Crane! Suddenly people were everywhere. Apparently, the gates of the zoo had been opened and many people were walking through the zoo for exercise or as a shortcut to another street. I followed the flow in the direction of what I presumed would be the entrance gate I had passed in the darkness.

I was shocked after leaving the zoo. Streets that had been almost empty were now jammed with traffic. Sidewalks were so covered by blue-suited pedestrians that it was impossible to run. Somehow, in the confusion, I made it back to the hotel, jumped in the shower, then threw on my suit just before the doorbell rang. It was Ding, Zhou, Liu, and an interpreter. "Dr. Archibald, did you have a good rest?" If they only knew…

A PAST LIFE?

One afternoon, I was thrilled by the opportunity to film the displays of the Black-necked Cranes at the Beijing Zoo. During my filming, an argument developed among the colleagues that joined me for the tour. Apparently, filmmakers from Hong Kong had filmed Golden Monkeys at the zoo, and sold the footage to the BBC for a handsome profit, none of which came to the zoo. Without paying, why should I be allowed to film the rare Black-necked Cranes? They asked that I stop filming while they had a meeting in a nearby building to resolve the problem.

I waited with my interpreter Annie Fu beside an old aviary containing a small group of Great Bustards. Alone for the first time, with tears streaming, Annie told me how she had been tortured at the zoo during the Cultural Revolution, and how many of her closest friends had committed suicide. She expressed the pain I had been sensing behind her smiles and warmth all week. Suddenly my problem of not being able to film the cranes seemed minuscule. Moved by Annie's words, I gazed blankly into the aviary of the Great Bustards, a species I had never seen before. Then a most remarkable thing happened. I had a strange feeling of deja vu that I had previously seen this enclosure and these birds. How could I have?

The Beijing Zoo of today was once the private menagerie of the Imperial Family. Many of the stone facilities for the animals had been unchanged for hundreds of years. Could it be that in a former life I was a keeper of the cranes in this Imperial Compound? Did the spirit of a Chinese zoo keeper resurface in rural Nova Scotia, link again with cranes in Alberta, and finally through ICF cycle back to that cage in Beijing Zoo? Or, was I simply tired, upset, and imagining things? I've held onto that mystery. Soon my colleagues returned and invited me to continue filming the Black-necked Cranes. Apparently, they recognized that my cheap Super 8 camera could never capture images of much value.

KEEP IT POSITIVE!

Most of my time in China that week was spent in the meeting room of the Institute of Zoology where colleagues were pleased to tell me that a major nesting ground for Red-crowned Cranes in northeast China was in the process of being protected at Zhalong Nature Reserve, but they had little information about cranes in other regions. Throughout the week, I gave a series of lectures at the Institute of Zoology about endangered cranes, storks, and ibis in nations that bordered China with the hope that my description and color slides of cranes in other nations would help the Chinese determine where to search for their cranes.

Based on what Ron Sauey had learned about the aquatic needs of Siberian Cranes in India, I felt it was urgent that their wintering grounds in China be discovered and protected. I was also concerned about the Crested Ibis, a species that had recently been extirpated from the Korean DMZ and for which only a half-dozen birds survived in the wild in Japan. Were there any in China, and if so, where were they?

Before leaving, I presented the scientists with stacks of color photos that could be mailed to colleagues in probable areas where Siberian Cranes or Crested Ibis might be sighted. When I continually expressed my concerns about the Siberian Cranes and the Crested Ibis, Dr. Cheng responded with the acronym "KIP" and a hearty laugh, meaning "Keep It Positive!" Dr. Cheng was thrilled by our week of communication, a week during which the ornithologists had a view of birds and the status of ornithology and conservation in neighboring nations. But I was seriously concerned. During the next year, I had several letters from Dr. Cheng telling me that the search was continuing. He felt my anxiety, and always ended his short letters with a KIP. Sure enough, a year later Ding and Zhou discovered the Siberian Cranes at Poyang Lake, and Liu found seven Crested Ibis in a remote valley of the Tsingling Mountains of Shansi Province. In a telegram soon after these historic finds, Dr. Cheng wrote, "We found 200-300 Siberian Cranes, and Crested Ibis. KIP really works!"

INTO THE FIELD IN CHINA

In the far northeast of China, the newly established Zhalong
Nature Reserve wanted help with field research and with equipment for their
new headquarters building constructed by the Ministry of Forestry beside
the great marsh. By collaborating with a Massachusetts-based organization,
Earthwatch between 1981 and 1984, 12 teams of volunteer researchers from
the U.S. studied the avifauna of the Zhalong wetland and more than $200,000
of materials were provided for the new research center. In exchange for one
pair of Black-necked Cranes from the Ministry of Forestry for ICF, we
provided seven pairs of cranes of foreign species of cranes to their education
center at Zhalong. My primary colleague at Zhalong was biologist Su Liying,
who later became the wife of Jim Harris, ICF Senior Vice President.

During those early days at Zhalong, government officials insisted on
accompanying us on early morning forays in the field to study the cranes and
other birds. Birding in groups of 20-30 is not ideal, especially when most of

the participants would rather be sleeping. But one must do what one must, so off we went returning in time for lunch where beer followed by a nap was necessary for the officials. Abstaining from strong drink, and after the nappers were asleep, the birders and I escaped to look for birds. It was not surprising that no one complained when we returned at dusk.

The Zhalong wetland is an enormous inland delta fed by the Wuyu'er River and ending in saltpans. In spring, it was a staging area for hundreds of Siberian Cranes and the largest known nesting area for Red-crowned Cranes in China. Near the headquarters, we were thrilled to see White Ibis, Spoonbills, and Purple Herons flying up from the reeds in a nearby area where they nested.

Perhaps a dozen Red-crowned Cranes and a few White-naped Cranes were kept in small enclosures at the headquarters. Hatched from eggs collected from wild cranes, and raised by humans, these cranes were tame and unafraid of humans. They were released from their enclosures each day for visitors to appreciate. Using food as bait, they flew over the wetlands and were trained to return to their pens. Some of the male Red-crowned Cranes were highly aggressive and somewhat dangerous for visitors.

One evening I returned to the headquarters and noticed one of these aggressive males had jumped the fence to enter the pen of his neighbor. The neighbor crane was afraid and pacing. I brought this to the attention of Su Liying. Without hesitation, she entered the enclosure, fearlessly grabbed the aggressive crane and gently placed him back in his own pen. To this day, this remarkable woman has been one of the leaders in crane research and conservation in China.

Ding Wenning and Zhou Fuchang of the Institute of Zoology in Beijing discovered about 200-300 Siberian Cranes at Poyang Lake, in Jiang Province late in the winter of 1980. They also discovered that local people killed cranes and other waterfowl by shooting shrapnel from cannons affixed to flat-bottomed boats that were silently blown by the winds within range. The hunter, covered by blankets, hid in the bottom of the boat and when the cannon was in position, dropped his cigarette butt into the gunpowder. Many birds were killed and wounded by a single explosion.

Ding and Zhou presented their findings to the provincial Bureau of Forestry and urged that the cranes be protected from hunters, and that the wetlands at Poyang Lake be protected as a nature reserve. In 1984, Poyang Lake Nature Reserve was created on paper. In 1985, in company of twelve ICF members, I finally visited Poyang Lake to see the Siberian Cranes, and to discuss conservation measures with both provincial and federal authorities.

ABIGAIL'S TEARS

It was a cold and foggy afternoon when the ferryboat finally reached the village of Wucheng on the north end of a long narrow island along the west side of Poyang Lake. Our facilities were unheated and the cold dampness went to the bone. Two elderly and white-haired members of my team, Fred Ott and Abigail Avery, were also members of ICF's Board of Directors. The press and more than 30 government officials joined us to find the Siberian Cranes.

Poyang Lake is China's largest freshwater lake. Pear-shaped with a neck that joins the Yangtze River, water from smaller tributary rivers flow into Poyang in spring and summer when the rains raise water levels. When water levels drop, wide expanses of mudflats are exposed and shallow "winter" lakes form in depressions. The edges of these winter lakes provide preferred feeding conditions for Siberian Cranes. In ankle deep water, the cranes excavate fleshy tubers and invertebrates from the mud.

The next morning I asked my colleagues where we might go to see the Siberian Cranes. No one seemed to know. Apparently both the birds and the borders of the winter lakes moved with the winds. Through popular consent, I became the leader of this large group of foreigners and Chinese who were searching for the elusive Siberian Cranes. With no knowledge of the location of the ephemeral winter lakes, I asked the captain of a large fishing boat to transport us southwest along a river that cut deeply through the mudflats adjoining Wucheng Island. Once again, the fog was dense. Even if visibility was better, views of the mudflats were blocked by the steep riverbanks. After about an hour of staring at banks, I asked the captain to put us ashore. We climbed the muddy banks and gazed into the fog and cold silence. In the distance, I could see the faint outline of Wucheng Island. It became our destination.

In her late 70s, Abigail Avery was the most senior member of the team. Trim and physically fit with snow-white curly hair and a wrinkled face, whose lines testified to decades of sunshine and happiness, Abby was right behind me. In a nation where the elderly are revered and pampered, the Chinese were fearful that at any moment Abby might collapse in the mud. She outdistanced them all.

It was noon before we reached Wucheng Island, and everyone was tired from slogging through the wet mud. After lunch and a rest, I imagined that I heard the distant calls of cranes from the west. Perhaps a mile down the sandy beach between Wucheng's hills and the mudflats, a narrow point of land extended from the island into the mudflats. It was our next destination.

By mid-afternoon, crawling in a horizontal line on hands and knees up a steep grass-covered slope, we approached a point of land that extended into the lake. Gazing down the other side was a breath-taking spectacle of hundreds of Siberian and White-naped Cranes and thousands of geese feeding along the edge of the winter lake. The sun was burning through the swirling fog creating warmth for the body and food for the soul. We were mesmerized beyond words. The birds were so close, and there were so many of them.

Sliding back down the hill, we gathered to discuss next steps and decided that a count was in order. Glancing at Abby, I noticed she was weeping quietly. Aware that her soul mate and husband, Stuart, had recently passed away, I put my arm around Abby and comforted her for a moment. Then I said with strength, "Abby, I need your help to count those cranes." Within a few moments, we were atop the hill with Abby making a stroke on the page

MY LIFE WITH CRANES

every time my binoculars reached 100 Siberian Cranes. To our amazement and delight, we recorded 1,400 – a thousand more than previous estimates.

It was late in the evening by the time we arrived back at Wucheng where dinner and cold rooms awaited us. After dinner, a faint knock came to the door of my bedroom. Two young and beautiful Chinese women, both journalists, wanted to know if it was appropriate to ask Mrs. Avery a question. I assured them questions were acceptable. We went to Abby's room and they asked why she wept after seeing the cranes. She replied, "I wept for joy. Just imagine so many cranes when we feared the species was almost extinct."

In China, where the elderly are respected as reservoirs of wisdom, the number 1,000 and cranes both have special good luck significance. I mentioned that solid line of white cranes feeding along the shoreline was like a great white wall. Soon, newspapers throughout China heralded that an elderly woman from Boston traveled all the way to China to look for cranes, and wept for joy when she helped discover 1,000 more cranes than previously were known to exist. The writer also loved the analogy of the living Great White Wall of Cranes. I have always claimed that Abby's tears did more for conservation in China than all of our research!

Cranes in the Outback

In northern Australia, an elderly indigenous man, Rowley Gilbert, lived on the land of his ancestors on the west side of the Gulf of Carpentaria. During the "Wet" of 1984, when I came to his homeland to study cranes, we became close friends. He shared with me the tragic story of his people. In his childhood, Rowley recalled living on the land with no contact with Europeans. Neighboring tribes were often hostile, but he remembered happy times hunting in the bush and feasting, singing, and dancing at their campfires under wide skies dotted by bright stars.

Brolgas were once found throughout much of Australia. In the south where the climate is more temperate, the colonists drained the wetlands and planted crops. European predators such as fox and house cats established themselves in the wild and ate young cranes. Habitat loss and predation led to the demise of the Brolga over most of its former range in the south.

In contrast, the intense heat and the floods of the Wet rendered northern Australia poor for crops, but excellent for beef cattle. Ranches sometimes stretched for hundreds of miles, and rivers more frequently marked their borders than fences. Within the ranch country, the wilderness remained, although the soils and the vegetation were markedly altered by hooved mammals on a continent where the soft feet of marsupials had evolved to spare the fragile soils. Seasonal wetlands created a plethora of places where cranes could breed. Some wetland plants survived the prolonged dry season by producing fleshy tubers that seemed lifeless in the parched soils until awakened when the rains returned. These tubers are the primary food of Brolgas during the "Dry." Huge flocks of cranes gather at areas of tuber abundance.

As a student of the evolutionary relationships among cranes, I was fascinated to know more about the interactions of Brolgas and Sarus in Australia. In 1972, I had studied both species during the Dry on the Atherton Tableland where I followed about 150 Sarus and a few dozen Brolgas. The two species were often together in flocks. They fed primarily on waste grain, reptiles, and rodents in recently plowed cornfields. Not far away on coastal wetlands, thousands of Brolgas and a few Sarus fed on tubers on the dried wetlands. It appeared that during the dry season, the Brolga fed primarily on tubers and the Sarus fed in open upland areas on seeds and small animals.

THE WET

My mission in 1984 was to study the two species on their breeding grounds during the Wet. In addition, I hoped to collect incubated eggs of both species to bring back to ICF headquarters for hatching, rearing, and research. At the time, Sarus were known to be extirpated from Thailand and they had not been rediscovered in neighboring nations. We proposed providing stock from Australia for a reintroduction program into Thailand.

Torrential rains close the roads in northern Australia from January through March. It is a time when many of the ranchers visit friends and family in southern Australia and those that remain repair machinery and saddles in preparation for the next season of cattle roundups. In mid-January, I landed in Alice Springs on a commercial flight and inquired how I might get to Normanton. My inquiries invariably resulted in incredulous stares followed by laughter. "You bloody bloke, don't you know about the Wet?" Undeterred, I continued my investigation and was finally able to convince a bush pilot to fly me to the northern outpost. Landing in Normanton between storms, the pilot introduced me to his friend, Sergeant Neville Travis Jones, the administrator of law and order for a fair portion of the coastal lowlands. A lady that owned a bed and breakfast welcomed this visitor during the off-season and provided delicious mangoes that she had frozen during the previous fruiting season.

Everyone knew about cranes, but no one knew the difference between a Brolga and a Sarus. Were they all Brolgas, or all Sarus? Cranes were in the backcountry but all roads were flooded and impassable. It was the season

MY LIFE WITH CRANES

when the enormous and extremely dangerous saltwater crocodiles migrated from the ocean up fresh water streams inland to breed. Could I escape from this frontier town, and if I did, would I escape the hungry croc? Recently the groom of a pair of newlyweds had been taken by a croc while sitting under the stars around their campfire near a river.

Normanton was truly a frontier town. Most of the locals had gone elsewhere for the Wet. Only a few hundred people remained in a town that boasted a landing strip and a main street bordered by the bush. The Purple Pub was a popular spot, and ringleaders of recent fights populated the chain link jail behind Neville's home. It was at the little church in Normanton that I met Rowley Gilbert. He told me the best place to study cranes was at the Delta Downs Station – his ancestral homeland and one of the stations that had been purchased by the government for the aborigines. "Em messes of Brolga over there," he said. He suggested that I ask Neville to take me there between storms in his police plane. It was only later while living with Rowley at the station that I discovered he knew the difference between the two species of cranes.

Soon Neville and his little plane brought me into the heart of crane country. The station manager, Bill and his wife, who had been hired to teach the aborigines ranching practices, welcomed me to stay at their home. Several aboriginal men and one woman, the cook, remained at the station throughout the Wet. Several days after my arrival, Rowley and a few aboriginal men walked out of the bush. One of these men, Roy Beasley, seemed interested in my work, and I hired him as my guide on the agreement that ten dollars would be provided for every crane nest he helped me locate. It was one of the best investments I ever made. He introduced me to the cranes and to life in the bush.

SEARCHING FOR NESTS IN THE BUSH

Every morning after a hearty breakfast of steak and eggs, Roy and I headed off on foot along one of several dirt roads that fanned out from the headquarters to various parts of the station. Although readily used by motor vehicles during the Dry, these roads were impassable during the Wet. Forests, savannas, wetlands, ponds, and streams bordered them. Lush grasses sprang from the previously parched soils, and most wetlands had one or more pairs of nesting cranes in a ratio of three pairs of Sarus to two pairs of Brolgas.

The Sarus appeared to prefer flooded savannas where scattered trees provided shade for their nests. Brolgas also used such habitat, but more often, they nested in the open wetlands where there was little or no shade. Neighboring pairs often performed their trumpet-like duets at each other to announce their defended real estate. Brolgas were often observed driving Sarus away from their breeding territory, and vice versa. There appeared to be a balance between the two species as they competed for the wetland breeding sites.

Every day I felt privileged to experience the wonders of the Australian bush and to have an aboriginal guide to teach me. Roy's eyes and ears were amazing. He could spot the red comb of a crane in the tall grasses half a mile away. We would then stand motionless with our backs to a tree waiting for the head and neck to reappear. In such a position, it is difficult for animals to notice humans. Within a few moments or perhaps as long as a few hours, the lone crane would return to the nest to relieve its mate of incubation duties, or the incubating bird would stand to turn the eggs. In either scenario, the nest was easily located. Within three weeks, we had discovered 75 nests from which I brought back to ICF two dozen Sarus eggs and one dozen Brolga eggs.

Colonies of noisy Magpie Geese nested in heavily vegetated areas of deep open wetlands. Scattered pairs of the black and white Rajah Shelducks brightened streams and ponds. The magnificent Red-shouldered Parrots were common in the savannas. An enormous male bustard, or bush turkey, selected the runway at the station as his display area. Saucy bowerbirds scolded whenever my path led too near their elaborate and arched bowers meticulously formed from twigs. Once, a male Red-winged Wren landed on a shoot of grass just a few feet from me. Sometimes, the hollow boom of the emus carried through the bush, and on a few occasions, we sighted these large flightless birds. Grey Wallabies were everywhere and occasionally we spotted small groups of gigantic Red Kangaroos. But it was the water that held our attention – not only for cranes, but also for crocs!

Roy had the greatest respect for crocodiles. Whenever we approached water of sufficient depth to hide a submerged croc, he diverted our path. On several occasions when he found the tracks of a croc in the mud, he described the size and the potential threat of the animal. Once we observed a pair of cranes at their nest on a small wetland just across a deep but long billabong. Roy took a chance and started wading across the open water. Foolishly, I followed. Suddenly Roy disappeared. Only his gray felt hat floated on the surface. Panic-stricken that he had been taken by a croc, I headed back for the shore at top speed. But Roy had simply stepped over an unseen bank

beneath the water, and completely submerged. We considered it a warning, and walked around the billabong to reach that nest.

The heat, rain, insects, and leeches were all challenges. A broad-brimmed hat, t-shirt, shorts, and rubber flip-flops constituted my uniform. In a backpack, I carried my camera, notebook, binoculars, and a large plastic bag. Bare feet performed best in the wetlands. During deluges, I simply removed all my clothing, and placed them and my backpack inside the large plastic bag. Roy was amused by my strategy. Some protection from the wind and rain was provided on the lee side of a large tree. The deluges, wind, lightning and deafening thunder gave me great respect for how the aboriginal people survived in the bush during the Wet.

On dry land between rains, temperatures sometimes soared to 115 degrees Fahrenheit. The evaporation from the wetlands cooled the water down by as many as 10 degrees. Consequently, I preferred walking barefoot in the water. Pressure exerted on the muscles of my ankles to keep my bare feet moving through the mud caused my ankles to swell grotesquely until the muscles grew strong. My forearms and the calves of my legs, both unduly exposed to the intense sunshine, blistered into hundreds of tiny welts. Outer layers of skin were soon shed and replaced by a toughened surface.

Usually the water was too hot for leeches. However, if I walked under the cooler shade of a tree where cranes often nested, I was attacked by enormous leeches and escape was possible only by standing on the nest like a crane. The sodden vegetation of the rapidly decaying nests smelled putrid in the humidity. A host of vicious insects swarmed around the nest to extract blood from the comb of the incubating crane. My bare legs were targets for cuts,

MY LIFE WITH CRANES

bruises, and insect bites. At night after bathing, the burning pain from dozens of little injuries from my knees down tortured me until fatigue rapidly propelled my escape into the land of dreams. By morning, the pain had disappeared and I was ready for the usual hearty feed of steak and eggs.

At each nest, I floated the eggs to determine their approximate age. Freshly laid eggs sink and lie flat on the bottom. As the incubation process continues, the eggs lose water and an air chamber at the large end of the egg increases in size, and the eggs become progressively more buoyant. A week-old egg floats vertically with the pointed end touching the bottom. At approximately two weeks, it floats to the surface. I wanted to collect the required number of eggs during their final week of incubation, a demand that necessitated locating a minimum of 12 Sarus nests (24 eggs) and six Brolga nests (12 eggs) that were due to hatch at approximately the same time. From the 75 nests located, approximately half were due to hatch within the desired period. The government had kindly provided an electric incubator, and during my last few days in the field, I tried to revisit all clutches of eggs selected as candidates for collection. Roy recalled the way back to every single nest. To my amazement and alarm, many of the eggs had disappeared and several nests were flooded and abandoned. Eventually though, we collected the required number of eggs.

Neville Travis Jones consented to transport me and the eggs in his small twin-engine plane from Normanton across the continent to Sydney. By phone, Mrs. Jones had made reservations for three seats on flights from Sydney to Madison, Wisconsin. Two plywood boxes lined with a shelf for hot water bottles and two layers of cupped Styrofoam created 18 little chambers in each box for the 24 Sarus and 12 Brolga eggs.

On our flight across the continent, one of the eggs hatched. After spending the night in an incubator at the Taronga Zoo in Sydney, several more eggs started to peep. With one egg box on a seat on either side of me, I embarked upon the long flight across the Pacific Ocean. Two more cranes had hatched by the time we landed in Hawaii. A Styrofoam picnic basket became the nursery. As each chick hatched, it was slipped into one of my socks. I cut off the toe end to allow the chick to extend its head and neck from its new home. Crane chicks can be extremely aggressive with each another. The socks solved that problem.

There were complications with the import permits in Hawaii. The officials firmly stated that I had permission to import eggs but not birds. So I was locked in a room until a few calls to Washington resolved the dilemma. The two boxes of eggs and I were released just in time to catch my connecting flight to Los Angeles. On this flight, several soldiers returning from duty in Korea shared many laughs. Each time their voices lifted, hatching cranes tried harder to escape from their eggs. Then while making a transfer to another airline in Los Angeles, someone stole my 600 mm lens. Finally, exhausted after 48 hours without sleep, I arrived in Madison. I passed my precious cargo – 31 eggs and 5 chicks to staff from ICF. That autumn, three pairs were transported to Thailand and presented to the Queen, as the beginning of what we hoped would be a reintroduction program in Southeast Asia. It was later determined that the Australian Sarus was genetically distinct, so the birds were not released into the wild in Thailand. Yet these cranes aroused great interest in bringing back Sarus to Thai wetlands.

Rowley and Roy, my close aboriginal pals were illiterate so it was impossible to communicate with them by written correspondence. In 1996, I returned to the Delta Downs station to repeat my surveys of nesting cranes. In addition, I wished to introduce the renowned writer Peter Matthiessen to the two species of cranes and their remarkable habitat. Peter was writing a book on the cranes of the world. With my recorded and mental maps from 1984, I led Peter and Australian naturalist Andrew Haffenden along the trails Roy and I

had traversed in our search for crane nests. The heat and humidity were so intense that Peter labeled one of our treks, the Death March. The cranes were still there in abundance and the balance of three Sarus nests to two Brolga nests continued to hold. Unfortunately, Roy had moved on, and Rowley Gilbert had passed away. On his tombstone in the little cemetery near the headquarters read an inscription, "Rowley Gilbert. Please do not forget me. Remember, I'm only a dream away."

A GIFT FOR A THAI PRINCESS

In November 1984, I greeted Princess Soamsawali as she stepped from her large white luxury limousine in Sriracha, Thailand. As she emerged from the car, I heard a loud whoosh-like sound behind me. I turned around to see thousands of Thai people on their knees with heads bowed to the ground. Not familiar with the tradition, I was surprised and then concerned that I was still standing. But the Australian Ambassador next to me assured me that all was well. I was witnessing the traditional prostration when encountering a member of the Royal Family of Thailand. The grand occasion was the presentation of eight Sarus Cranes raised at the International Crane Foundation to the Government of Thailand. The government had built excellent facilities for the cranes at the Bangpra Waterbird Breeding and Research Center. We hoped it would be the beginning of a captive breeding center that would allow the reintroduction of cranes to Thailand.

I walked behind the Princess as she slowly made her way through the throngs of people, bending down along the way to speak softly to the many upturned smiling faces. They adored her. In a large colorful tent, VIPs had assembled to greet the princess. She sat in an adorned chair at the front of the gathering to listen to a number of speeches. I didn't understand a word of it. After the ceremony we walked along another path to several rice fields that had been flooded to create what looked like a large pond. A new

walkway over the water led to a canopied platform where the princess, the ambassador, and I had some moments for conversation, while across the water the cranes foraged in their newly created aviaries and the mass of people awaited the return of their princess.

We had tea and sweets, and I told her about how I had first met Thai colleagues at a crane workshop in India the year before. They had told me how the widespread conversion of wetlands to farmland and uncontrolled hunting had spelled the demise of the Sarus Crane in Thailand. But since that time, laws had been created to protect endangered species and new wetlands had been created — just waiting for cranes to return. That was when I realized I could help them bring back cranes to the landscapes of Thailand – so, the return of the Sarus began on that day at the elaborate presentation of cranes to the princess. At first, the whole event seemed like such an over-the-top exhibition to me, but I soon realized that because the princess was so beloved, the cranes would garner the same adoration from the people of Thailand. It was a brilliant public relations move by my Thai colleagues!

Fast forward to August 2016 when I received a letter from Ms. Nuchjaree Purchkoon of the Zoological Parks Organization of Thailand announcing that for the first time ever, four pairs of Sarus Cranes had laid eggs in the wild of Buriram Province. The reintroduction began in 2011 at the Korat Zoo where approximately 12-15 juvenile cranes are reared each year. An idea that hatched in India in 1983, seems to be coming to fruition 33 years later.

DANIEL DOLPIRE

Making Friends in Africa

In the 1970s and 1980s, the International Crane Foundation's work concentrated on the critically endangered cranes in Asia. Our work in Africa started in the late 1980s, bloomed in the 1990s, and continues as a major focus to this day. My first trip to Africa was in 1985 to attend a meeting in Francistown, Botswana of the Pan African Ornithological Congress, an organization founded through the suggestion in 1954 of Dr. Cecily Niven of South Africa. The first meeting was in 1957. The one I attended was the sixth, and Cecily always sat in the front row taking notes. We became fast friends.

Cecily was the daughter of one of the founders of South Africa, Sir Percy FitzPatrick. In 1959 she founded the Percy FitzPatrick Institute for African Ornithology at the University of Cape Town. Today this Institute is one of the leaders in ornithological research worldwide. Meeting Cecily was a golden opportunity to discuss how the International Crane Foundation might best help the cranes of Africa. After hearing my presentation, Cecily had one suggestion. I must meet Lindy Rodwell in Johannesburg. A few days later Lindy and I met. At the time she had established a small business for which she created and sold lovely ceramic dishes featuring colorful paintings of wildlife. She was not a birder but had a great interest in nature and conservation. At the time, she was also dating Cecily's grandson.

A few months later, Lindy was a summer volunteer at ICF working mainly with the Education Department. We shared many discussions about the African Cranes and put together a newsletter to send to African colleagues, featuring information about African cranes that ICF had received in recent years. She returned to South Africa inspired to help the cranes, and that led to employment at the Endangered Wildlife Trust and the genesis of a program now passed from Lindy to Kerryn Morrison and called the EWT-ICF Partnership.

ADVENTURE IN BOTSWANA

One of the greatest wetlands in the world is the Okavango Delta in the Kalahari Desert of Botswana. From the highlands of Namibia, the Okavango flows southeast toward the heart of the continent. It spreads across the sands creating an enormous pie shaped wetland. Papyrus swamps in the deeper northern portion and shallow ephemeral wetlands in the south, with surrounding islands of savanna, provide habitat for a diversity of wildlife from crocodiles to lions, from Carmine Bee-eaters to Wattled Cranes. On the southern border of the Okavango, the little town of Maun provides a jumping off point for thousands of visitors who fly into isolated camps throughout the Delta. Maun was the site for the Wildlife Training Center of Botswana, the venue for ICF's African Crane and Wetland Training Workshop in August of 1993.

For several years prior to the meeting, I journeyed to Maun to develop plans for our historic gathering that would include about 100 kindred spirits from Africa. Arranging a field excursion into the Okavango for the delegates attending the workshop was one of the objectives of my visit. Although hippos and crocodiles could be easily observed in the Tamalakane River and Wattled Cranes along the Boro River just northeast of Maun, I wanted everyone to experience the more remote areas with the unique feeling created by untouched wilderness and its profusion of wildlife.

The Khwai River flows into the Delta from the east through an area once controlled by tribal chief, Moremi. The Moremi Wildlife Reserve is known to support the greatest numbers and diversity of wildlife. But how does one bring more than 100 delegates to Moremi? Surely, we would never be able to afford the expensive tourist lodges. Would camping be too dangerous? I wanted to find out. A government officer drove me from Moremi to the few

huts that constituted the headquarters of the Moremi Reserve. He left me in the hands of a red-haired, Setswana speaking, enthusiastic Peace Corps volunteer, Jeff Burn. Jeff was excited to meet someone from the homeland and he wanted to show me everything.

That night, I pitched my tent under a huge bat-filled tree between Jeff's hut and the Khwai. At the campfire, Jeff told me a fascinating stream of stories about life in the wilds of Africa. About 20 feet from the campfire, the bright stars were blocked by an enormous mass. A bull elephant was watching me. Hippos snorted as they emerged from the wetlands into the grassy areas between my tent and the water. As I rested on the little metal cot in my tent that night, droppings from bats sounded like fat raindrops striking the tent.

During the night, I was awakened by a continuous roaring from the west. It was strong winds. When they struck, a few limbs from the tree above me crashed to the ground and the vertical flaps of my tent were suddenly horizontal, as wind and sand blew across the interior of the tent. I had been lazy and did not properly secure the stakes of my tent. My brief case had been placed in the sand beside the head of my cot. As I heard it sliding, I jumped from the bed to grab it, but it disappeared into the night. Somehow, I found a flashlight and I traveled with the wind in quest of my case.

Fortunately, it had lodged against the trunk of a tree. I struggled back to the tent fearful that I would never find my glasses that I left on top of the case. After many moments of groping in the dark with sand and debris blowing into my face, I was unable to locate my glasses. I am nearsighted and not having my glasses would be disastrous. I would not be able to conduct my work without them. Knowing that it was a futile investigation, I opened my brief case and there they were! Was I witness to a miracle? The wind died as quickly as it had arrived. I secured the tent and with my glasses in the briefcase and my belt anchoring the briefcase to the metal bedpost, I slept soundly.

The next day, Jeff introduced me to his world. We traveled east into the Delta and delivered supplies to workers at a remote ranger station. Prides of lion, herds of elephant, ungulates of many types, leopards in a tree, pairs of Wattled Cranes here and there along the Khwai provided a visual feast for the eyes. It was late in the day when we finally headed back to base camp. Soon we were driving in darkness.

About seven miles from camp the Land Rover stopped. Out of gas. "Perhaps we should remain in the Land Rover all night," I suggested to Jeff. "Oh no, that's much too dangerous. Elephants play with lone vehicles and unfortunately I neglected to bring a gun." Recalling that most animals are afraid of fire, I suggested we make a fire in the clearing in the forest. In almost total darkness, I raked leaves and twigs with my hands into a pile surrounded by bare sand. Some flames rose as larger sticks were added. The fire was a success that required my constant attention as it was the dry season and I didn't want it to spread. Jeff and two other colleagues remained near the Land Rover. Apparently, by shaking the vehicle, some gas became available and the vehicle started. But before I could join them, they roared off down the road leaving me alone with the fire in a wilderness of hungry predators. Jeff had reasoned that if they stopped, the vehicle might not start again, and we couldn't leave a fire unattended in the forest.

There I was, alone in the forest with only a fire to offer protection. I was filled with fear. I summarized a "what if" list that included the arrival of an elephant, buffalo, lion, leopard, hyena, crocodile, hippo and wild dog. Most of these I thought could be avoided if I climbed a tree. So, with a large club in hand I tried to become comfortable high in a large tree about 30 feet from the fire. Every 20 minutes I climbed down to fuel the fire. Perched in the tree after a few hours I found it difficult to avoid sleep. I prayed for my safety. The

only sound I heard was the gentle cooing of a dove. Around midnight, Jeff returned and took my photo after I climbed down from the tree. For him it was a great joke. For me it was confirmation that Moremi should not to be a destination for participants attending the Africa Wetland Training Workshop.

TOM LYNN

Reflections

THE SPIRITUAL SIDE
OF THIS CRANIAC

Eleanor Roosevelt once said something to the effect that birth and death are mysteries, and she didn't know which one was the most fascinating. I agree. When one gazes into a microscope or the night sky, there is a type of infinity in both directions. Here we are in the middle! It's such a mystery. Raised in a Christian home, my personal beliefs are based on what I was taught and subsequently experienced. Working in such a diversity of cultures and religions, I have been curious about the beliefs and personal experiences of my many friends, all the while maintaining my foundation in Christianity. Perhaps my most treasured conversations were with the well-known writer and Zen Buddhist, Peter Matthiessen, with whom I worked for a decade on his book about cranes, *Birds of Heaven.* He and I both held that a spiritual world exists that humans lack words to describe, but with effort, we can connect through religion. For Peter, it was a type of Buddhism; for me, Christianity. For both of us, things did not seem to happen in a random way. There was unseen guidance. There are many deeply personal things that I hope to someday share, but the time is not yet ripe. But I will share two accounts that involve cranes and spirituality. The first concerns a Siberian Crane chick, the second a Whooping Crane.

In 1981, we hatched the first Siberian Crane, Dushenka, from an egg laid by captive cranes. That same month, an Indian colleague Prakash Gole was a guest at ICF. Fascinated by our prairie restoration project and the philosophy of conservationist Aldo Leopold, Prakash and I had long conversations about conservation in India. When some of the challenges in India seemed overwhelming, I would end by stating, "In our weakness, He is strong. Place your problems in the loving hand of Jesus Christ and expect a miracle." Prakash sighed.

It was a gorgeous spring morning when I drove Prakash to the airport. We stopped to see Dushenka. I asked Prakash to hold the little crane for a photo.

He was hesitant but I insisted. Sure enough, after I clicked the camera, the chick jumped from Prakash's grasp and lay unconscious on the pavement. Horror of horrors! It was a disaster and it was entirely my fault. A gifted chick mama, Marion Hill, gathered up the chick and took it to the nursery with a smile that she was convinced it would recover. I prayed to God for guidance to comfort Prakash. On the drive home from the airport the gravity of the situation took hold of me. I needed to pray. I stopped on a small country road, parked my car under a tree, and listened to a cassette of a sermon on tithing. I thought it was just a time-filler, because I already tithed. However, the final words of the sermon were "When you have done all you can, place your problems in the loving hands of Jesus and expect a miracle." It was the advice I had given to Prakash. Next, I felt myself losing consciousness and I grabbed the steering wheel. Suddenly all was darkness from which a cloaked figure appeared and picked up a little Siberian Crane chick. Then I awoke still grasping the steering wheel. The first thing I saw was the face of my watch. It was exactly 3:00 p.m. I felt a great peace. Dushenka was either dead or recovering.

It was 4:30 p.m. when I arrived at ICF. I parked my car and waited while three colleagues approached and told me that Dushenka regained consciousness at 3:00 p.m. For the next three days and nights, I was with that crane chick encouraging him to drink, putting bits of food down his throat, and gently supporting him to stand and walk. Healing came rapidly. Within a few years and then for several decades, Dushenka was one of the most productive Siberian Cranes at ICF.

MEETING JOHNNY CARSON!

And miraculous things happened the following year in connection with the long-shot hatch of Gee Whiz, the Whooping Crane chick resulting from my unusual courtship of Tex. Three weeks after the hatch, I was invited to tell the big story on the popular *Johnny Carson Show*. I flew to Los Angeles the day before the taping. Before leaving Baraboo, I had one last dance with Tex in the enclosure and the big grassy field where we had first danced six years before. The following morning in my hotel, I decided to read the book of John in search of a scripture that I could write on a card and place in my shoe so I could stand on the word of God. I was concerned that my story with Tex might make me the laughingstock of the masses. I needed spiritual strength!

Then I found my verse from John 7:37, "If anyone is thirsty, let him come to me and drink." I wrote it on my card. The phone rang. It was Joan Fordham, ICF Administrator. "George, I am so sorry to tell you this, but last night Tex was attacked and killed by a pack of raccoons." Shocked, I returned to my Bible and read John 7:38, "Whoever believes in me," as the scripture said, "streams of living water will flow within him." Deeply affected by the strange timing of Tex's death, the upcoming stress of appearing before 22 million people, and with tears flowing, I wrote the second verse on my card. Johnny Carson, Ed McMahon, and Doc Severinsen could not have been more considerate. At the end of the 15-minute interview, I explained the tragedy. The studio audience groaned, and throughout the country, there was a new awareness of the plight of cranes. It has always worked for me to literally stand on the word of God!

THE DEPARTURE GATE

Much of my life is spent in travel. Airports and airplanes are my churches. I have a special memory of an airport incident that gives me great comfort. It is the story of a pilgrimage to Pittsburg to visit the church and office of the late evangelist and faith healer, Kathryn Kuhlman. The visit happened at the end of an exhausting lecture tour to twelve universities in the span of two weeks. As I sat in a pew of Ms. Kuhlman's large Presbyterian Church, I did not feel anything special. So, I went to her offices where some elderly ladies gave me tapes, books, and warm wishes before I left for the airport. My funds were dwindling and I had less than $2.00 remaining in my pocket. After making a collect call to ICF, I bought a cup of coffee, and sat watching the masses of people bustling to and from flights. Suddenly I noticed a well-dressed man stop and stare at me. He approached me, stood there, and said, "During my flight, I had a vision of you sitting there. God told me to tell you that he loves you very much." I was so surprised, that I blurted out, "Well, God bless you too!" Then he departed.

MY LIFE WITH CRANES

CRANES ARE MY PASSPORT

Recently my assistant Karen had a large stack of my old passports on her desk. She diligently typed up the list of countries I visited from 30+ years of passports. As I looked through the list, it reminded me of so many stories, from so many faraway places, over so many years – enough to fill volumes. Cranes truly are my passport!

Countries Visited

1980
Japan
South Korea

1981
Dominican Republic

1982
Japan
South Korea
Saudi Arabia
India
Saudi Arabia
China
UK
India
Pakistan
China
Japan
India

1983
Japan
Singapore
India
UK
Japan
China
China
India

1984
Thailand
Australia
India
India
China
Thailand
Japan
South Korea

1985
China
Japan
Japan
Rep South Africa
Australia
Botswana
UK
Japan

Hungary
China

1987
China
Hong Kong
Japan
China
Japan
China
Hong Kong
Japan
China
Thailand

1988
Hong Kong
Vietnam
Thailand
Philippines
Hong Kong
Kenya
England
Nigeria
Botswana

1989
South Korea
Thailand
Vietnam
Finland
England
South Africa

1990
India
Thailand
Vietnam
Thailand
Japan

1991
France
Pakistan

1992
Thailand
Vietnam
Cambodia
Thailand
Pakistan

Botswana
Kenya

1993
South Africa
South Africa
Botswana

1994
China
Mexico

1995
Russia
Japan
South Africa
Botswana
Zimbabwe

1996
Thailand
Australia
India
Nepal
Japan
India

Thailand
Germany
Bhutan
India

1997
Belgium
Russia
South Korea
Japan

1998
India
Germany
India
Thailand
Bhutan
Thailand
Bhutan
Iran
South Africa
England
Nepal
India
Thailand

Bhutan
India
Germany

1999
Nepal
Thailand
South Korea
India
Iran
Bhutan

2000
Russia
China
India
Bhutan
Japan
Thailand
China
Cambodia

2001
England
Singapore

Japan
Mexico

2002
Vietnam
Japan
South Korea
China
China
Thailand
Afghanistan
Japan
Bhutan
Iran
Ireland
India
Russia

2003
South Korea
Japan
Germany
Mexico
South Africa
Zimbabwe

　　　　　　　　　　　　　　MY LIFE WITH CRANES

South Africa
Botswana
Zambia
Japan
Thailand
Bhutan
India
Afghanistan
Germany
Iran

2004
China
Russia
Russia
South Korea
Thailand
Bhutan
India
China
Iran
Thailand
Afghanistan
Pakistan

2005
China
Japan
China
South Korea
Russia
South Korea
Thailand
Pakistan
Cambodia
Russia
India
Thailand
Nepal
Bhutan
United Arab Em.
Pakistan
Afghanistan
Azerbaijan
Iran

2006
Mexico
Russia
Pakistan

United Arab Em.
Germany
Bhutan
Pakistan
Japan
South Korea
Thailand
Nepal

2007
Germany
England
Kazakhstan
South Korea
Thailand
India
Nepal
Bhutan
United Arab Em.
Germany
England

2008
South Africa
China
DPRK

South Korea
Japan
Russia
Japan
Japan
South Korea
Bhutan
Thailand
Norway

2009
Thailand
India
South Korea
Japan
India

2010
Iran
Thailand
Japan
Russia
Bhutan
Belgium
Italy

Germany
Thailand
China

2011
South Africa
Botswana
Zimbabwe
Uganda
Kenya
Rwanda
China
Japan
Russia
South Korea
Russia
Germany
Bhutan
Thailand
DPRK
China
DPRK
South Korea

2012
Ethiopia

Japan
Russia
Mongolia
England
China
DPRK
Thailand
Bhutan
China
South Korea

2013
South Africa
Botswana
Zambia
England
Mongolia
Japan
Bhutan
Thailand
China
DPRK
South Korea

2014
India

Vietnam
Cambodia
Japan
Russia
Mongolia
Australia
Thailand
Turkey
England
Germany
Spain
China
Japan
South Korea
DPRK

2015
Ethiopia
Mongolia
England
Belgium
Switzerland
Germany
Russia
Canada
Bhutan

India
China
South Korea
Thailand
DPRK

2016
Mongolia
Ethiopia
Canada
Bhutan
Germany
Czech Rep.
UK
Switzerland
France
Thailand
DPRK

TRANSITIONS

At the millennium, I reflected on the new century and what it held for cranes, for me, and for those who had been with me since the beginning of the International Crane Foundation's journey. How would the leadership move forward – with me or without me? I knew that founders could become liabilities. After 27 years of leadership, it was time for me to assume a new role and it was also time for new board leadership. Mary Wickhem had given 22 years as Chair of our Board of Directors without missing a single meeting. Mary was a disciplined and powerful force. She had also become a close personal friend and we probably both knew deep in our souls that it was time for new leadership and growth beyond us. I proposed to Mary that we step down together but continue active involvement, myself continuing on staff and both of us continuing as board members. I assumed the role of Interim Chair. After two years of feeling ineffective and disliking the position, I passed board leadership into the capable hands of Joe Branch. It was a new era. Mary and I sat together at board meetings and began to watch great things happen.

Jim Harris, my excellent Deputy Director, became the President and CEO. I moved my office to my home but continued to work full-time in a role that involved fundraising, leading group trips to wonderful crane landscapes, spearheading new programs in Ethiopia, Mongolia, Bhutan, and North Korea, and helping the staff, without micro-managing or undermining the new administration. My overriding goals were to help the team through encouragement, financial security, and when asked, advice.

And there were less altruistic considerations as well. I expressed my need for close association with birds by expanding my flocks of chickens, turkeys, peafowl, guineas, and pigeons at my farm. I never realized how stressful administration was until I was no longer administering! Long hours in the office, stacks of mail to master, constant calls, special tours, and meetings, consumed my life during those 27 years of leadership. I enjoyed my work, but there was just too much of it. I will always be most grateful to my personal assistants who organized me through those hectic years. Being somewhat driven though, I found myself just as busy as ever, but in a different way.

THE SEVENTY MILESTONE

Now as I turn 70, I have thoughts about my future path and wonder what is ahead. Many of my most meaningful conversations have taken place in nature. Last spring, I talked with Tim Tuff among the prairie chickens and sandhills in Nebraska. Tim has been a close friend since our university days at Dalhousie University and is now a productive member of our board of directors. His advice for this new chapter: "Do some things you really enjoy." I have thought about Tim's kind words and concluded that my greatest happiness is when I am helping others in the presence of cranes.

Reflecting on these experiences, I am reminded of five days a few years ago out in the field with ICF's Griffin Shanungu at Lockinvar National Park in Zambia. Together we watched 800 Wattled Cranes feeding on the seed of ripened grasses. We talked about the future of these cranes and the many that would leave their fledged juveniles as they moved on from that huge congregation. Sharing my knowledge of Wattled Cranes with Griffin gave me the kind of joy Tim Tuff was talking about. I have been blessed with knowing many kindred spirits throughout my life and my vision for my future is time in the field where I can share, learn, and develop ideas with old friends and new kindred spirits. To continue my work and dreams we must invest in the conservation leaders of tomorrow. I will continue to work toward that end, in the persevering Scottish way instilled by my parents.

I am sometimes asked if I am thrilled with the success of ICF. Thrilled is not the right word… I have moments of a warm glow that the dream of two college kids has matured beyond their wildest expectations, but as long as I am alive, my overriding thought will be of keeping the engines running and of the programs that will continue long after I have joined Leopold's cranes in some far-off pasture of the Milky Way. The dream is still in progress and I have faith. I always have.

SANDI WHITMORE

AFTERWORD

Determined Dreamer

By Rich Beilfuss, President and CEO, International Crane Foundation

I first met George Archibald not in the exotic wilds of the Australian outback, or while dancing inside a crane pen, but in the middle of a parking lot at the International Crane Foundation. The year was 1988, and I was a young Civil and Environmental Engineering graduate student at the University of Wisconsin-Madison, just back from a year in Nepal, and searching in earnest for a meaningful thesis project that would send me back overseas. The latest *ICF Bugle* featured a cover story on George's recent trip to Vietnam, where Eastern Sarus Cranes had just been rediscovered for the first time in 30 years in Vietnam's war-torn Mekong Delta.

The unfolding story in Vietnam – about the need to restore a great wetland to save an endangered species – captured my imagination and career ambitions, in one fell swoop. I had committed to a summer internship to get to know the International Crane Foundation's conservation work and had already developed a great passion for ICF's accomplishments and a great admiration for George. As I strolled toward George in the parking lot, trying to catch him before he reached his pickup truck, I summoned the courage to make my pitch. I greeted "Dr. Archibald" and hastily blurted out my name, background, and life dreams in about 30 seconds. A big smile spread across George's face, and he said, simply, "Sounds great, why don't you do your thesis with us in Vietnam and develop a water management plan for Tram Chim?" Within a few months I was on the ground in Vietnam, and thus was born my (now more than 25 year) relationship with the International Crane Foundation.

Over the past 43 years, George has offered such unqualified encouragement countless times in countless places to countless strangers and colleagues alike. In our mission statement we call this "providing knowledge, leadership, and inspiration." But first and foremost, it is about encouragement. And no one on the planet excels more at encouraging others than George. Throughout his career, George has stayed up into the wee hours of the morning answering every letter (now email) he receives, from professional colleagues to schoolchildren to hopeful graduate students like me, full of ideas and just needing encouragement, a bit of advice or direction, and a sprinkle of hope. For many of our fellow "craniacs" working in isolated regions, this connection makes a world of difference – strengthening the resolve to fight on another day.

The wonderful stories George has shared here capture the exciting and extremely challenging early days when he set about building ICF from a graduate student dream into a world center for the conservation of cranes and their ecosystems, watersheds, and flyways – one crane at a time. He ventured into exotic, almost forbidden places like China, Russia, Iran, and North Korea to discover crane populations and nurture the local passion needed to save them. He triumphed over daunting setbacks – the tragic loss of Ron Sauey, losing half the captive flock to an epidemic, losing his beloved Tex – setbacks that might have ended the journey for other, less-determined dreamers.

A recurring theme in George's stories is his role as a catalyst – getting things started and then passing projects to the capable hands of others to carry forward and succeed. Many of the initial efforts George describes – and many, many more since then—continue through the long-term commitments of the International Crane Foundation and our partners. Today, we work on five continents, with major projects in Asia, Africa, and here in North America. George's early work in Vietnam has blossomed into award-winning efforts to save Sarus Cranes and wetlands in the Mekong Delta, led by Vietnamese and Cambodian colleagues under ICF mentorship. The African Cranes and Wetlands Workshop in Maun, Botswana held in 1993, resulted in projects and relationships in 20 African countries over subsequent decades, a deep long-term partnership between ICF and the Endangered Wildlife Trust of South Africa, and major conservation impacts in Zambia, Mozambique, Uganda, Rwanda, Kenya, South Africa, and Ethiopia. George's time in Japan back in 1972 jump-started power line marking and wetland protection that revived the Red-crowned Crane flock from a low of about 170 to more than 1,800 birds today – now in the capable hands of Japan's Red-Crowned Crane Conservancy. Our efforts in the Korean Demilitarized Zone, and the dream to reunite Korean scientists through "conservation diplomacy" based on a mutual passion for cranes, continue to this day. Gee Whiz, the remarkable offspring of George's long courtship with Tex, grew into what is now a sixteen-year partnership to reintroduce a second flock of Whooping Cranes to the eastern United States, and our commitment to safeguarding the original wild flock of Whooping Cranes that migrates between remote Wood Buffalo National Park in Canada and Aransas National Wildlife Refuge on the coast of Texas. And on and on we go.

Today, George's passions are divided among diverse places such as Bhutan, North Korea, Mongolia, Yakutia, Ethiopia, and Turkey, inspiring the next generation of conservation leaders in all of these places. He also devotes considerable effort to fundraising to help ensure we can continue to support and empower these leaders in the places that matter most to us (while also helping us keep the lights on).

Even a dreamer like George could never have fully imagined what ICF would become. A robust headquarters in Baraboo, Wisconsin dedicated to visitor education and outreach, cutting-edge crane husbandry and captive breeding, field research on cranes and wetlands, conservation leadership training, and so much more – all led by a passionate group of 50 plus staff and many more associates, interns, and volunteers. Our international programs and teams are now based in China, Russia, India, Vietnam, Cambodia, South Africa, Zambia, Uganda, and Texas, with a worldwide reach to fellow "craniacs" in more than 60 countries. Our projects serve as conservation models (some of them award-winning!) for strategies such as sustainable water management, land protection and stewardship, biodiversity conservation on agricultural lands, and market-based solutions for conservation-friendly livelihoods.

ICF's 43 years of achievement are the product of many, many talented and dedicated staff, partners, and volunteers. The world of ICF extends far beyond what George could ever have dreamt of. Yet so many of our fellow Craniacs still trace their conservation roots back to a catalytic spark of encouragement from George. That is a conservation legacy that George should be very proud of, and for which the world should be very thankful.

Triet Tran

Acknowledgements

My Mother

My beloved Mother, Lettie, was a MacLeod from Heathbell, Pictou County, Nova Scotia, Canada. Her parents were dairy farmers who tilled land pioneered by ancestors in 1805. The eldest of five, only two years separated Mom from her sister, Christine. They were best friends throughout life. They always walked the two miles each morning to the one-room school where

they finished the first nine grades before boarding in Pictou to finish high school at the Pictou Academy – the first of its kind in the province. Mom worked after school as a maid to support herself. When the results of the tough provincial exams were revealed, Mom was the only one who passed Grade 12. Holidays were spent at home on the farm helping with the harvest and attending the United Church of Canada in nearby Scotsburn.

Victor Bakhtin

Mom attended Normal College in Truro and then taught in a one-room school in Rockfield, a rural community near Scotsburn. A hobby farmer in Rockfield, Don Archibald who milked a few cows to supplement his income as a math teacher at the high school in New Glasgow, met Mom at church. They waited for some time to marry until Christine found her own mate. "I didn't want Christine to feel left out," Mom once confided. Mom and Dad raised six children, Anne, George, Don, Heather, Sandy and Peter. We lived on the farm in Rockfield until 1954. I have fond memories of preschool days when Mom and I were home alone. Every afternoon we shared a nap on the kitchen couch with the cat!

Mom loved to visit her many friends. With a car filled with kids, she would go from farm to farm chatting in the kitchen with the housewife over tea and cookies, before moving on to the next farm. While Mom made the rounds, we played with farm kids and explored the barns and the animals. Mom taught me the power of communication by keeping in touch through short visits and personal letters. She was also an excellent and faithful writer of letters to family and many friends.

On a frigid winter day in 1954, our home in Rockfield burned to the ground. Soon we moved to Guysborough County. During the fishing season, Dad spent many a Friday night and Saturday in the woods at his camps, while Mom managed the household and tended her many flower gardens. Decked out in rubber boots and old overalls and crouched on the ground, she often spoke sweetly to her favorites and scolded the weeds! I inherited my love of gardening from my mother. Mom had a special gift for handling animals. At Grandpa's she could manage a huge workhorse that others considered violent. After a cow freshened, Mom talked to her, and then milked her when she refused to stand still and relax for others.

Mom was sincerely thankful for so many blessings. It always inspired me how "up" she was, alone in her house after Dad died, sometimes snowbound, and more than a mile from the nearest neighbor. Don Frazer, a cousin and a mechanic in Sherbrooke, drove up every evening to see if Lettie's lights were on. And during the day, friends were often visiting the great matriarch whose optimism and joy were contagious. She undoubtedly had the greatest influence on my life. And now, for more than three decades, I have been an active member of only one public organization, the Baraboo Optimist Club!

Outstanding ornithologists who have inspired me include:

Dr. Jean Delacour, a French aristocrat and ornithologist, studied birds in Indochina when much of the area was under the control of France. In 1931, he authored a volume, *Les Oiseaux de L'Indochine Française,* followed by seven more volumes about birds. On his estate he raised many cranes. He had a remarkable sense of humor. In 1979, he visited the International Crane Foundation. Walking slowly with the aid of a cane, he crossed the lawn to greet an aviculturist who was exercising four Red-crowned Crane chicks. Aware of how aggressive hand-reared cranes can become as adults, he commented with a twinkle in his eyes, "One day those birds will want to kill you!" Needless to say, the crane keeper was startled.

Dr. Roger Tory Peterson, or "RTP" of Peterson Field Guide fame, was a member of the Board of Directors of the Cornell Laboratory for Ornithology when I was a graduate student. Adverse to meetings and addicted to observing and sketching birds, I often found him sketching my cranes. And he visited Baraboo when my *Cornell Cranium* in New York transformed into the International Crane Foundation in Wisconsin.

Sir Peter Scott was a painter, author, naval officer, co-founder of the World Wildlife Fund and founder of the Wildfowl & Wetland Trust in the UK. He and his lovely wife, Philippa, visited ICF in the early years when we were located on the Sauey farm. He was thrilled to see captive cranes released from their enclosures, circle high in the sky and return, something he had done with waterfowl at his home in England. Peter dreamed of having cranes one day at the Wildfowl Trust. He passed away in 1989, twenty-four years before the Wildfowl Trust became the center for costume-rearing Eurasian Cranes for release into the wild in western England.

Another co-founder of the World Wildlife Fund, **Dr. Luc Hoffman,** visited the new International Crane Foundation to speak at our Annual Meeting of members. Dr. Hoffman, from the Swiss family of Hoffman La-Roche, founded and directed for many years the Tour du Valet in southern France, a research center for the conservation of Mediterranean wetlands. In 2015, I was the guest of Dr. Hoffman at his home in France to discuss plans for perhaps the rarest and most endangered bird species of Asia, the White-bellied Heron that I have been helping in Bhutan for the past decade.

Sir David Attenborough is just as charming in person as he appears on television. In 1997, he spent several days with a film crew at the International Crane Foundation in Baraboo to capture the costume-rearing of cranes for a television special, *The Life of Birds*. It was a unique opportunity to become friends with a man I had admired for decades. When I asked him what his favorite television story was, he immediately replied *Attenborough in Paradise,* which documented his experiences with some of the beautiful and unusual Birds of Paradise. Subsequently, he sent me the DVD and within a few years, I had shared it with so many friends that a replacement was necessary. In 2014, I visited David at his exquisite home in London. It was 2:00 p.m. and he answered the door with hair uncombed and barefoot. He had been up all night with a film crew at the Natural History Museum filming a new show about dinosaurs. At 87, he was as youthful and joyous as always. I will always cherish the memory of my two visits with this great man who has done so much to bring to millions the beauty and value of nature.

Thank You

I thank my parents for encouraging my interest in birds and my wife, Kyoko, for her steadfastness and delicious meals for the past 35 years. Without my fellow co-founders, Ron Sauey and Forrest Hartmann, and the generosity of Ron's parents, Norman and Claire Sauey, the International Crane Foundation would not have happened.

My gratitude is extended to my devoted personal assistants who in chronological order were Marie Oesting, Eric Scott, Teresa Searock, Susan Finn, Julie Zajicek, and Karen Becker. After I served as President for 27 years, subsequent leaders Jim Harris, Jim Hook, and Richard Beilfuss led the organization's growth. When the Board of Directors was expanded in 1978, Mary Wickhem became the Chairman and served for the next 20 years followed by Joe Branch, Hall Healy, and Jim Brumm. Their leadership and the support of other members of the Board has been vital.

I extend a special thanks to Charlie Luthin for initiating our prairie restoration, to Konrad Liegel for planning our new site, and to Bob Hallam for his leadership in raising funds to support our work around the world. I am also grateful for all of the staff, volunteers, and supporters over the years. Finally, I wish to thank my friends from many nations for their commitment to the welfare of cranes and for adding so much color to these stories.

The creation of this book was made possible by editor Betsy Didrickson and her helpers, Karen Becker, Liz Pelton, Carol Fleishauer, and Emeritus Board members Richard Steeves and Sandi Whitmore.

BOOK SPONSORS

The second printing of this book was made possible by a major gift from Mary "Tinker" Callen.

Design and production was made possible through the generosity of the Willis G. Sullivan, Jr. Family, Carmen Mockrud, and Bob Hallam.

In 2012, I was humbled and honored to be inducted as a member of the Order of Canada, which recognizes outstanding achievement, dedication to the community, and service to the nation. It was presented by Governor General, David Lloyd Johnston, on behalf of Her Majesty Queen Elizabeth II.